*IN AND WITH THE BEGINNING*

# IN AND
# WITH THE BEGINNING

A Wider-eyed, Open-minded Look
at the Conscious Life

Alastair Hannay

humming earth

Published by
humming earth
an imprint of
Zeticula Ltd
Unit 13
196 Rose Street
Edinburgh
EH2 4AT
Scotland

http://www.hummingearth.com
admin@hummingearth.com

Text Copyright © R. Alastair Hannay 2020
First published October 2020


Cover image: *Raum* (2000) by Friedel Anderson

ISBN 978-1-84622-077-7

## *ACKNOWLEDGEMENTS*

I owe to my searching grandmother and thoughtful parents a background of open-mindedness that, for good or bad, has outlived the necessarily narrower focusing of an academic career.

There, I owe much to the writings, both sceptical and inspiring, of colleagues, among them in particular Paul Feyerabend, Ted Honderich, Vincent Hope, Gilbert Ryle, John Smythies, and Timothy Sprigge.

I owe a special debt to W(illie) F. M. Stewart, my excellently erudite teacher then in Edinburgh, whose positivist leanings were tempered by an unusually, and today untypical, detailed knowledge of philosophy in the round.

# CONTENTS

# FOREWORD

The ideas discussed here were aired in a recent novella in which the thoughts, uncertain existence and possible death of its protagonist are the theme of a troika of fictitious authors. *Hello and Goodbye, Horace Hardcover* was written under my name, but the perspectives there form a horizon wider than any I can claim as my own. Thoughts, like children, are sometimes better handled for what they are when separated from their origin. As though sent up anonymously in a balloon to find their sympathizing reader in some faraway place, those presented here are extensions of some sketched in that novella but here given a more scholarly look. Although the fictitiously elusive author's uncertain death is dated 1996, several supplementary references beyond that date have been added. A preface pleads with the reader to accept that, apart from purposes of cataloguing and reference, an author's identity is not so very important.

The undersigned nevertheless remains responsible.

*Borre 2020*
*Alastair Hannay*

# ANONYMIZING PREFACE

Drop the book and I'm gone. But, yes, a tag helps. I'm under 'Removal' – not the furniture but the drapes. 'Recovery' would do, but not with re-cycling in mind.

'What needs removing?'

The rust of words corroding a natural ability to note where and what we are, words that form their own order of things, words whose elegant orderings win approval from those who cherish elegance over truth, or words whose confinement to technical vocabularies takes truth out of ordinary hands. So, yes, a hammerer of rust, that's what I am. Like patina, rust can tell us of the depth of time, but both are literally superficial and get in the way.

'Of what?'

Of what's there.

'But it's there, too.'

I see you have done some philosophy! Well, take a breath. Let me explain.

Some time ago, yes it seems a lifetime, I was hired to look at this thing called 'philosophy'. Well, not really, I looked in on it out of curiosity but gradually came to believe I had a cleaning up mission. No, not voices, just self-administered pep. They say you can't decide to believe things, not really believe them since then it's only your own preferences at work. That's what they say, but believing what you want to believe is also a basic urge that sweeps such niceties aside. In my case it was not belief but disbelief that made me messianic. I could not, for the life of me, believe what I heard the philosophers saying. It took a long apprenticeship in their practices and thinking habits to realize what their words actually meant, and as you would expect it was not as simple as my incredulity had assumed. By the time I had acquired the required techniques I realized somewhat to my relief that not only philosophers but also philosophies came and went – the latter quite quickly. In my early apprenticeship it was no obstacle to philosophizing that one knew little or no science. Any argument depending on facts of any size was dismissed as irrelevant for the truths we were after. These were called 'conceptual'. I learned that much that was wrong in our thinking was due to confusion in this area. To clear the way forward philosophers had found it necessary to devise concepts of their own, new words that map our ways of thinking and talking. Today, less than a generation later, it is quite the opposite. Whether neophyte or veteran, any thinker openly controverting articles of current scientific faith is an outcast – unsurprisingly now that philosophers have taken on the task of drafting the latest creed.

Yes, apprenticeship. Whatever philosophers like to tell you what philosophy is, you cannot properly understand it without extensive mind-on experience in whichever part of its landscape you find yourself. Like many of my confederates, I began on the shop floor, read widely, took degrees and even set off hopefully on a career. Befriending many of the discipline's exponents along the way, some of them star performers, a competitive urge led me to do some desultory dabbling – or was it just babbling? – of my own. I even beguiled an editor or two into publishing some suitably packaged thoughts. In brief, inspired by the technical fluency of my colleagues' minds and their contagious enthusiasm for verbal disentanglements and questions about questions, I too became an enthusiast of sorts. Indeed, so infected did I become by the sheer glee of those engaged in this captivating intellectual pastime that I began to lose sight of the very suspicions that first led me to doubt its credentials. Perhaps it was my upbringing or some innate romanticism and a pre-Nietzschean exposure to religion. Whatever the origin, instead of unpicking the tapestry of words with which professional philosophers seemed to obfuscate disturbing matters of human concern, I now found myself plying still more threads to their already intricate weave.

Worse than any sense of being untrue to myself in this pursuit was losing sight of a self I might be true to. In one way it was what professional philosophizing can do to you, but in another it was a result my professional colleagues were quite ready to applaud. Under their laser gaze, that you and I have or are selves was one of the first myths to be exploded. What could any self be but a grammatically induced illusion owing to the native ability of any normally equipped adult to grasp and employ the first-person pronoun?

There was more to come, or more exactly to go. Even an illusion must exist but where? In the mind of course; that is where illusory ideas are formed along with all else we talk of – where else? The mind also forms, among other things, ideas of itself, and many of these ideas too are very likely illusions. The Greeks had their elements and our grandparents believed that we have wills free enough to choose between the paths of perdition and salvation. Such are the images that the mind has of itself through time and formed under the influence of ideas not garnered exclusively by attending to the basics of its own domain. Extraneous ideas like these may be unavoidable. They are in any case there, or rather here and with us as part of the energizing contents of our minds.

Psychologists once unpacked that convenient but diffuse term 'mind' into what we can be seen to do. The philosophers, more reluctant to dispense with the privacy of conscious life, plotted its logical relations to something clearly public, namely language. 'Mind' could go public by being the ways in which we actually use a vocabulary of mental words but not always in their popular senses – this owing more to 'folk psychology' than to science and prone to producing a popular 'psychobabble'. Today, people with laser eyes fixed on the brain tell us that far from being the powerhouse that drives and directs our conversations and mutual doings, and in whatever way we catalogue its contents, 'mind' too is just the brain's invention.

Neurobabble? Am I to believe that in venturing out on the busy street to put my latest job application in the post I am being frogmarched there by the play-in-concert of very small things of which I know nothing and of whose doings I find no compelling reason to call my own? Since – if you insist on talking in this way – I am also 'going quietly' albeit urgently, I find it incredible that I am not somehow engaged in this everyday manoeuvre as *myself.* Making the world with which we learn to be familiar so totally spectral would make an image-maker even as adept as Jean Baudrillard dizzy.

To my despair at being selfless in a sense that gave me no moral credit was added a disorientation in which all that could keep me on my feet was a sneaking suspicion that this surely could not be what the intra-cranially erudite could really mean. Like the good David Hume, the fact that when exiting a room, they too choose the door rather than a fourth-floor window demonstrated a shared disposition to believe that a body 'has gravity and can be injured by a fall'. It is a tendency activated in the presence of alternatives that they see and respond to, and that it is *they* who respond. [1]

## STREAMS AND CONSCIOUSNESS

As Goethe's Faust is borne heavenward the chorus proclaims: 'All things transitory are but parable'. Events in the phenomenal mind may seem about as transitory as anything. Scientific custodians of the mind have for well over half a century been busily pointing to this evanescence. Their philosophical gatekeepers have been even more vociferous. Power-point presentations replace careful observation and introspective awareness. We are led to believe that the mind is best seen in the ways we observe it at work, and listen to ideologically tuned theories on how that happens. Writers exploiting the 'stream of consciousness' have provided convincing proof from even further back. How could any such succession of disconnected images, memories, reminders, passing twinges and aches support a theory that affords a grip on whatever it is we call the 'mind'?

Is it possible that the confusion in what passes in the conscious mind is exaggerated? We will look into that. We need to since there has been a fair amount of road-show rhetoric encouraging us to turn our attention elsewhere. Introspection, even in the time of its exemplary nineteenth-century exponents, suffered the stigma of subjectivity in a world of science understandably protective of its well-worn rule of thumb: 'you show me and then I can begin to believe you'. The fact that Francis Galton's detailed 'result' showing how scientists tend to be weak in mental imagery has been disclaimed indicates the fragility of such examinations,[2] while its non-occurrence in some people puts the phenomenon itself well back in the queue for inclusion in general theories of mental activity.

That will not deter us in what follows. Our focus is on a different narrowness. Where the response to the unfashionable privacy of introspective psychology was a tradition of behaviourism that deliberately ignored subjective reports, the current reaction is to a confinement of studies of the mind to the complexities of that very particular thing we all have: a brain. There are different ways in which such a study may seem inhibiting and in need of some loosening up. We have exponents of the 'Extended Mind' who see those afflicted by defective memories achieving with written rules the same goals as those with their memories intact. Think of a trip to the moon by an astronaut whose careful training was lost with the shock of lift-off yet managed the landing with a book of procedures. There would still be plenty for the brain to do or have done, creating the spacecraft for instance, even if a computer program once devised could do that too. The point, it seems however, is not to show that the actual states of mind of a trained astronaut and one forced literally to do it by the book are the same, but that information can be applied in both these ways in the service of a goal. [3] We (but still our brains) contrive make-shifts in the form of *aides memoire*, shopping lists, check-lists, road maps and – why not? – even a chart of the universe, that lighten the burden of the brain's memory and attention functions. The liberating thought is that we think not just with the brain but with these visible prosthetic aids. In doing so we (or our brains) make a part of the world our own.

But liberation can be sought in another direction. We can all grant that this hugely complex organ must be firing away as we move whether thinkingly or unthinkingly. Advances in the understanding of the intricacy of its workings are made every day. And yet to suppose, as some do, that our conscious lives are best deciphered without serious reference to what enters the conscious mind is not only counter-intuitive but unnecessarily, let us say, demure.

There are reasons for being shy. Frustrated by a scepticism that puts the pre-brain-processed world out of cognitive reach, and even makes the world we think we know and share into a private show, to point out, as mind extenders do, that the world is what we think with, is as welcome a release as that 'naturalizing' of epistemology that places theorizers unproblematically in the midst of things. It lets them get down to their business of data collection and theory-spinning. [4]

What pinches now is their narrow theory-driven focus on the brain. Reductive materialists claim that anything a neuroscience cannot in principle explain is of no theoretical interest. Any evidence of an inner life too obvious to overlook is treated as a superfluous spin-off or a free rider. Decorative pendants to the inner workings that philosophers call 'epiphenomena' don't actually do anything. When all is said and understood, the conscious life is analogous to the exhaust an internal combustion engine expels when the job is done, or in an organic context excrement. In a kinder metaphor, it is there just for the ride. Any specious sense of active engagement merely indicates a smooth co-ordination of the functional parts.

There is no getting away from evolution even if in other contexts what look like *ad hoc* attempts to save a paradigm normally spell 'pseudoscience'. Here, the likelier reason is that besides on-going disputes about the mechanisms that drive evolution, more is to be accounted for than still unidentified details.

Science in alliance with philosophy must be the judge of that. For us, in our untutored simplicity, it may help to look openly at our own minds in their everyday working and with only hand-baggage theory. We can open our eyes to what we find around us and find inspiration for understanding of what we are even there. You might be going for your well-earned weekend country stroll and when stopping on a bridge lean over the parapet to peer down at the flowing stream. It may put you in mind of what you might be.

As your eye follows the dark water downstream you see a liquid body following its own itinerary indifferently to the incidental ripples and gurgles dictated by the changing bed. Direct your gaze at any spot on the opposite bank and see how the stream becomes a passing parade of shimmering reflections, wavelets and floating twigs, interrupted only by a locally stable pattern of movement from some boulder or dangling branch. That stream of consciousness, the metaphor once so much in literary fashion, is born of this latter one-spot perspective. Looking in one place, all you see is either a series of images and disconnected or tangentially associated thoughts in the mind of a character. The stream looked at in this way is a darling of writers, an artifice of a style chosen for the writing itself.

In real life the 'stream' might be the random thoughts of someone lazing in a hammock without any attempt at sustained thinking. But what if the lazing is an occasion to think through something, for instance the present experience of gently swaying from side to side? Or after the weekend, take ordinary workaday dealing with life, getting up, washing, making breakfast and driving into town? Or a situation that calls for greater alertness to what goes on around: crossing a busy street.

The relevance of personal observation for theories of human behaviour seems fairly obvious, we do quite well with pains, wants and occurrent (as against 'dispositional') beliefs. Less so in making sense of the world 'out there', but without going to Goethean lengths, what appears in a careful and theory-driven inspection of experience may tell us something. For the feted German poet, bureaucrat and naturalist, it was the sight of a leaf as he wandered in an Italian garden; it gave birth to the *Ur-Pflanze* and became the cornerstone of a contribution to a natural science in which classifications and explanations are drawn from data available to the creatively observant eye. Here we may ask ourselves, more generally, how much creative observation of any kind, whether in science, poetry or just getting a good idea, depends on association in the realm of what we sense. If it does so depend, then how far beneath the conscious surface will we have to dig to explain how it is done?

But first the beginning.

## 'IN THE BEGINNING ...

... was the word'. John the Evangelist's own beginning uses more than one, but we seldom use a single word and when we do, it typically covers for more, as with 'Stop', 'Exit', 'Gap'. 'Danger'. The latter can say 'Better not go further'. But sometimes single words are not needed either. Perched unexpectedly at the edge of a precipice, the edge itself says enough.

Ever since their trade began, philosophers have asked about the relation of words to reality. Plato thought a fitting name would best capture it. Empedocles before him had found poetry the way to express life's important connections. In our own day a more prosaic proposal came from Ludwig Wittgenstein. A sentence is a picture of 'what is the case'. This very matter-of-factual proposal had its classic apotheosis in the *Tractatus Logico-philosophicus*, which begins by declaring that the world itself is 'everything that is the case'. [5] Let us bear that remark in mind.

Why John speaks of 'the' word can wait. First, we must find out how much can be said about experience without its dictation. Might we not respond to Wittgenstein and say: In that case it is not the word that is in the beginning but the fact that it helps to depict when part of a sentence? But then we will find ourselves asking, is it at all possible to look at experience 'as is' without a sentence in mind? Hasn't the world already done its own dictation before we start? Doesn't describing anything after all require words? Perhaps there is something already there in an experience telling us whether the words in the sentence *we* dictate make our sentences true or false? Maybe a 'canonical' language will meet and cleanly capture what first meets the eye. [6]

Perhaps, but the words used here are more like indications of what we may ourselves recognize in experience, rather than direct representations of what is recognized. They point to features of our experience that may at least first off seem as inherently dumb as in an unexpected encounter with the edge of a cliff. To Insist that the edge is, in a manner of speaking, doing the speaking may merely indicate that we are caught up in a prejudice endemic to philosophy and to that extent one of the profession's shortcomings.

Try then to forget the potentially gun-jumping schemata of philosophy and science. Turn to the world around you and see how far the basic divisions reveal themselves in your own experience even if, as here, vicariously. Start at the real beginning. Not with words, not even with what you see in front of your nose. Take a close look at your embodied self and you will find it also includes your nose.

# MY ABLE-BODY 'IMAGE'

Under the summer sky, swaying gently in a hammock in a light and cooling breeze, the leaves rustling gently above in the trees suspending it, I feel that I am in my body. Not like a pilot in a ship, as René Descartes is so frequently quoted as saying: the movements the vessel makes under the pilot's direction are too remote. The better image is of a hand in a glove. Especially when stretching I seem almost coextensive with my body. But now, with little else to occupy me, and as I reflect on this, I realize that not everything is how I might expect. For instance, the inside of my nose seems much bigger than it should in proportion to the rest, and my feet feel nearer than they seem to be when I look all the way down to my toes. I sense this because I know how human bodies look and are proportioned and am quite well acquainted in the same way with my own body – I've seen pictures of myself and there are mirrors and of course other people. Roughly speaking, from where I am, I feel like an indeterminate but roughly body-shaped and fairly well-defined area of space inserted somehow into that familiar much larger three-dimensional landscape that occupies what I catch sight of within my field of vision along with those nearby parts of the world I know very well surround me even if, just now, I cannot see them. In that part of the physical world associated with this inserted space that is visible in what surrounds me my toes can be seen beyond the kneecaps and these beyond my chest. Other signs of this surrounding space not perceptible in this way include small sounds. A squeaking of the rope behind my head is not associated with the space that I feel is partly myself. Beyond what I actually hear and see, there is also some kind of intimation of the familiar things I *would* see but at this moment can only hear, for instance the voice of the person setting the hammock in motion.

Even though the hammock is swinging I am quite still. When it sways I move too but, really, I am just as still as when standing stationary on the sidewalk watching the traffic while nevertheless moving with the earth's rotation, and for that matter even in its orbit around the sun, or in the course of some indiscernible seismic commotion. It is only in relation to my noticing that parts of the surround in which I am placed are shifting in relation to the whole that I mark myself off from everything else. Just now, as the hammock swings, and whether rocked by wind or helping hand, I see parts of the local surround disappear then reappear, disappear then reappear. In this 'stable me here/changing vista there' we glimpse the makings of a subject/object relation. More primitively it may be better described as a here/there distinction with a moving/unmoving feel.

The wind dies or the helping hand is removed and the movement slows, the difference a kind of interruption itself to be interrupted through my own body's exertion. As a settled state of soothing movement caused by something else, it seeks its own continuation. It so happens that I know which parts of my body to twist and what weight distributions to alter in order to get myself in the hammock swinging again. That is what I am now doing, combining what might loosely be called my own initiative with the dynamic possibilities of hammock arrangements.

Although not just passively swaying, am I now then able to say I am 'active' in the typically either/or sense used by philosophers? In this case there is at least no *choosing*. Either I somehow got the idea or it got me, and getting it was just about the same as the resumption or continuation happening: no legislative phase preceded an executive one. I could well have thought of it first, weighed up the pros and cons and then decided to keep swinging, but not this time. In fact (come to think of it!) I seldom do anything in that bureaucratic way. If incorrigibly given to 'how come?' thoughts, I might well reflect on the natural set-up that makes the motion possible and even go on to include other things, my own physical make-up for instance, and my brain and nervous system, and proceed even further to the absence of any hindrances to what these normally permit, such as numbness or paralysis. Just now, none of this occurs to me, at most the sense that the relaxing movements continue through my own effort.

If now asked *where* any thought of taking over from the breeze or helping hand might have occurred, I might in this case truthfully answer by saying it didn't seem to occur at all. But if pressed, I might say that if anything approaching a thought arose, it was somewhere between my ears. If you are to describe where thoughts *appear* to occur, that is what you will find it natural though a little odd to say. Reflecting on the apparent location of your thoughts as you sit there back in the cabin harking back to the hammock episode and trying to relocate the experience in a string of words as in the above, the thought that this is where the thought that you might have had, and now the one you are actually having, is located might even make you smile.

This is how it seems to you and ordinary common sense tells you it is the natural answer. But science will also say it is the right one. Between your ears is where these thoughts actually occur, but they will advise you to add that since between your ears is where you will find your brain, that organ is also where you would more precisely locate those thoughts. Well not exactly you, for that would require some complicated technology and tools, but an expert probing that brain with a scan or some suitable instrument.

Should science patronize common sense by telling it to take its at first hesitant answer to be true? Not about where the brain is, for neither is mistaken on that count, but about taking 'in the brain' to be an intelligible answer to the question of where that thought occurred to you.

# THOUGHT IN CONTEXT

Yes, where are my thoughts? Or more generally, how do my thoughts relate to this bodily existence of mine which is shared with others in a space of physical things? Thoughts don't fit easily into space talk; even if between the ears, they don't seem to take up any of that space, something Descartes noted but also, long ago, worried Aristotle too. Since others even earlier had also worked on it, a brief run-up to Alexander the Great's tutor can place some more cards in our hand.

Curiously, the topics that the study of mind has given rise to have resolved themselves historically (and not just in English) into an alliterative quintet: sentience, sapience, selfhood, semantics and that mysterious interloper the soul. Does the hissing of the sibilant 's' have something to do with it? Perhaps. From classical times we have also inherited 'psyche'. Linked to 'breathing' it became the sign of life. Then 'soul' came along in various material degrees and senses, its historical root having the sense of a binding or being bound. 'Spirit' was added to the list and, in myth as in Homer, it could appear in bodily shape. Christian theology later freed it from corporeal bondage and as the Holy Spirit it became sufficiently elusive to require recapturing by hearts sufficiently open to let it in.

As for the soul's 'binding', for ancients the idea came in various versions. For Empedocles, as psyche it was a fifth element holding the classic four (air, fire, earth and water) together, while for the atomist Democritus the world was composed of indivisible and therefore indestructible particles with shapes that held them together by themselves in ways specific to the element in question. Except, that is, for air, which was also slippery enough to escape Descartes' more recent dilemma of how such disparate entities as particulate matter and space-less thinking can influence each other without an intermediary that in some still inexplicable way has something of both. Descartes found a candidate in the brain's pineal gland whose function is still not fully understood. But air, for Democritus, by having nothing rather than everything in common with the other elements, could mingle with all the others. Carrying the thought of the psyche's pervasiveness in today's direction, came Aristotle's 'soul' as the functional shape of the body, its arms, legs and so on, the soul's 'form' being all that of which a human body was capable. However, unable to affix the ability of rational thought (*nous*) to any specific bodily function, Aristotle left a loophole for theologians and scholastics to exploit in the form of yet another 's': the survival of the destructible body.

It was perhaps the headier metaphysical speculations on that topic by his teacher Plato that cautioned Aristotle not to enlarge on this internal anomaly. Or perhaps it simply left him puzzled. Since the entire Aristotelian opus is itself a path-breaking product of *nous*, that is not surprising. One wonders whether, had current neuroscience been available at the time, Aristotle would have assigned this central human capability to the brain, pointing out that, in our thinking, that organ's patterned workings in some way exemplify *its* functional 'shape' or form.

Pure speculation of course, but even if he had pursued that line, there is still something more to account for, namely, and again, the phenomenal thought's problematically non-spatial location in space: not just where the thought itself might be, between the ears or in its own space, but also its spatial relation to the biological episode in which it occurs.

Philosophy is traditionally both by and for tidy minds but also bent on making untidy minds tidier. Those that it sets out to describe from scratch tend therefore to be tidier than those you find in normal life. Gottlob Frege, one of analytic philosophy's founding fathers, didn't see his job as that of investigating 'minds and the contents of consciousness whose bearer is the individual person'. That would be something for the psychologist or biographer. His interest was in getting to grips with 'Mind' itself, [7] a topic that we can grasp when far enough removed from our actual selves to distil a thought we can in principle share with others. What is left behind is a 'mode' of an 'individual mind', a 'merely' psychological event that he calls an 'idea', and from this perspective a mere idea, since in referring to it 'one must, strictly speaking, add to whom it belongs and at what time'. [8] For philosophical purposes that means it is destined for a refuse bin, one that an even tidier-minded philosopher who, in charting the assumptions we must make to be having an experience at all, had called 'inner sense'. [9]

Put simply, the idea here is that we must separate the thought – since at least Plato the medium of truth – from the psychological frippery that surrounds its occurrence. Like the smooth rock over which the constantly changing stream of consciousness flows, a thought if it is to be conveyed to others must stay the same – even more so if its representatives are to play a part in a universally valid formal logic.

We may ask how often in the course of a normal day thoughts are conveyed whole, other than in newspapers, weather forecasts, timetables, telegrams and now the mind-shrinking social media? Conveyed whole, that is. What, after all, is a thought taken from the experience in which thinking it occurs? It would be hard in the semi-organized mess of any running commentary on an actual stream of consciousness to locate anything so simple or abstract as the sanitized thought that philosophers need when classifying and identifying formal relationships between propositions. Thoughts like these, laid out cold like fish on a slab and gutted of all 'psychology', are well suited to standing tests of inference and non-contradiction, but once sentences are made proxies for what occurs in the mind of someone thinking we can doubt whether philosophers and linguists or, more obviously but innocently logicians, are dealing in entities with any living semantic value at all. Semantic entities embody meanings, what someone has in mind and might want to convey in some particular context on a particular occasion. A meaning's true habitat is not a dictionary or a form of words but a situation where something occurs to someone or something needs to be said.

Language can at times be a poor medium, though the fault is sometimes due to a limited vocabulary. On the other hand, in order to capture the full import of any thought, widely conceived as what goes on in the consciously reflecting mind, you may have to descend to less conscious layers of meaning where the relations between meanings and intentions are murky. Re-surfacing at a linguistic level might require the creative gift found in and cultivated by poets if not also the elicitings of psychiatrists. But, of course, some thoughts are conveyable, and life could hardly go on without them. Netted from the stream of consciousness such thoughts perform the all-important function of passing on information. Someone comes up to me in the station and asks me the time, I glance at my watch and say 'It's twenty past one'. That is very useful, but unless that brief encounter becomes part of something more, a murder investigation for instance in which I am involved, it will not connect with the longer term and ever-churning traffic of my mind. Was it even a thought? What was it I thought? 'What a nuisance, maybe I will be late'.

## IMAGES THAT ARE

Of all Aristotle's predecessors, physicalist science resembles most the atomism of Democritus: the universe is composed of particles or, in their macroscopic form, what we know as matter. Often, the objection of physicalist science to those who insist on including experience or 'phenomenality' within the catchment area for relevant theory of mind, is that they postulate 'mental stuff'. Association with ectoplasm, auras and ghosts adds to whatever repugnance that idea can occasion in an age no longer fascinated with table turning and talking to the dead. But why talk of matter at all? Or rather, admitting there may be a question of strange matter, why should the prior problem not be that of a mental 'space' merely as such?

Back to the hammock. The helping hand was withdrawn. The slowing pendulum motion was corrected by small body twists and weight re-distributions. I know which parts keep this occupied piece of stretched canvas in motion. Unlike my toenails, they are parts I can feel, just as – if this party trick is in my repertoire — I feel my ears or at least the relevant muscles 'from inside' when I wag them. These felt bodily parts form locations in a roughly body-shaped envelope within which I and my physical body are located in the visible segment of the larger three-dimensional surround in which we live and can call our individual part of a wider world. There is talk of the 'sensory somatic field', but a metaphor conveying the sense of area and volume as well as circumference will convey better my able body's placement in the world as I feel I am in it. The idea is that of a uniform surround in which my sense of what lies invisibly behind me within my mental space and the sight before my eyes are both included. In spite of a theory-driven temptation to impose a sharp distinction between input from 'outside' and what is owing to the experience from ourselves, the steps behind you as you walk up that dark and lonely lane to the house ahead are, however imaginary, spatially continuous with the light shining from one of its windows – as far as the experience itself goes.

Although they inhabit a swathe of the same space with us, philosophers have done little in the way of space-theorizing. If not like Kant concerned with the conditions of experience, which of course include space, philosophy's analytic exponents stick to their topic: language. Faced with space they chart the distinctive 'grammars' of our various space-related ways of talking. There is talk of 'primal' space, 'neutral' space, even 'brute' space and a space that 'aspects' in many ways. [10] But an indeterminate space that lies behind its several modes of appearance is not the space of experience: it is a construction, a deduction, an inference, the first step towards puzzle-generating theory and several careers in philosophy. For us, however, sharing our space with them, this space is in its determinate reality the one space in which anything that can appear does so in its own way. Whatever on reflection fails to belong among its publicly locatable properties has nowhere else to be than in this unspeakable space.

Scientists can for their part play fast and loose with space both in the singular and the plural, they too can do this without having to look, even when they deal with perception. Their concerns propel them out of the phenomenal world into the dark of its unperceived causes and the space that we and they phenomenally inhabit falls unnoticed between two otherwise (pre)occupied stools.

What, then, *is* this proprioceptively apprehended volume that I am, or am in or somehow part of and my habitation of which resembles more a hand in a glove than a pilot in a ship? Among the answers that might occur to me is this: it is just what it seems to be, a spatial entity, three-dimensional at that. Or is the 3-D effect a trick of the brain? If so, I might ask whether these bodily movements in the hammock might actually occur *without* my really sensing the location of the relevant parts. Raising the question to a more general level, I might wonder whether some artificial sense of where my legs are located in relation to the sun-filled space I am presently occupying has nevertheless become essential to the performance. Phenomenality matters and my conscious self is involved in the mattering, or it is not involved but the phenomenality works by itself, so that I can ignore the sense, leaving it to the legs and their connection to my brain. Playing the evolutionary card, it can occur to me that this sense of inhabiting a body must after all play some biologically useful, even necessary, role in sustaining the behavioural system that I am. Isn't it reasonable to expect that I need this apparent intermediary just to get around? Can our sense of bodily ability really be just an evolutionary spinoff while the real workings are 'undercover' and accessible only to investigation from 'outside'?

In whatever way we answer these questions, there remains the phenomenon known as the body-image. Not the idea we form of our physique from a mirror, or an advertised ideal of how people should look, a body-image here is the actual 'proprioceptive' sense of my able-bodied self, however distorted it may be when compared with the actual spatial layout as otherwise determined.

Why, though, call it the body-*image*? It may seem the right thing to call a distortion of the actual proportions that an 'original' will be shown to exhibit. Just as a Picasso portrait misrepresents the way in which the model actually appeared to the artist, the way in which our immediate sense of the mutual distances between the various parts of the body can vary independently of actual physical changes suggests that this sense similarly delivers images. Amputees can feel limbs at distances from the nose when there is no limb to be felt. As we approach sleep, there are both magnification and shrinkage that we know not to be happening to our actual body. Images are *of* something, in this case, a distorted representation of this actual physical body, of the body I can look at and check whether the parts are still there and in their usual proportions.

In occupying the same space as his model, the image constructed by Picasso is nevertheless robustly real. Must we not therefore attribute some corresponding reality to the body-image, even if unlike a painter's canvas it may not be composed of particles and thereby count as (normal) matter? It is, after all, there – or, in so far as it is a very immediate aspect of what I am, should we perhaps say 'here? Indeed, am I not, myself, in some essential way *it*? Less the image *of* my body than my own directly apprehended able-body. Even if what I feel as 'being myself' in this proprioceptive way were somehow illusory, the private 'mirage' of my phenomenally able body is still there (or, more accurately, *here*). However much it is insisted that I am no more than a piece of automotive furniture in physical space together with this ability to locate its 'inside', this latter capacity is still to be accounted for.

Mental imagery has been a constant flea in the physicalist ear. If impossible conclusively to swat this importunate insect, it is imperative at least to ignore its presence and take for granted that the multi-layered brain does all that is needed. Putting the fleeting mental image sufficiently in the shade is no hard task. As a parasitic merely 'as if' seeing, a 'seeing' in brackets, imaging is easily brushed aside as secondary to the real thing and placed, if a little awkwardly, on the same shelf as pretence and make-believe. [11] But the threat it poses is great enough, as confirmed in a comment some years ago, that being able to dispose of these 'will-o'-the wisps' would be a case of 'good riddance'. Why? Because there is nowhere to put them: '[W]e can all do without the dimensionlessness [sic] of mental images and their penchant for inhabiting a special space of their own ...' [12]

But while the elusive mental image lacks the evidential clout to crack the armour of a physicalist science, the body-image is different. It stands, so to speak, on its own legs and resists this rather desperate *ad hominem* treatment. To all appearances, as just now swaying from side to side in my hammock, it is only by virtue of my proprioceptively apprehended three-dimensional living in this 'inner' space that I am able to keep it going.

The body-image might of course also be found some secondary role. It might be an 'extra' adding something to the performance or have something to do *behind* the scenes. It might be a device the brain itself has come up with for putting a finer edge on corporeal agility, or the brain's way of helpfully keeping an eye on what the active body is currently up to on its own, a kind of 'voyeur' role relieving it of the need of some 'undercover' surveillance of what 'really goes on'. Should that be unconvincing, and we agree to accept the auto-phenomenology of the animated body as at least the way things *appear* to the animated body in question, science still has a set of terms ready to encapsulate it. In a word borrowed from the philosopher's vocabulary, the body-image is said to be composed of 'sensa' processed in the brain. They are the same sensa as those said to form the wider sensory field in which the trees and the sky appear above my head. [13]

What more, then, need there be to the fluctuating body-image than this processing between my ears? Scruples about the whereabouts of the imagery can be dealt with by talking of the physical body being felt to have an integrity that it sometimes lacks, as in the case of that lingering amputated leg. For all normal purposes that is enough. Without risk of debarment, the scientist can allow 'the perceived body and its behaviour [to] belong to the same world as ... the visual field "with all its distances, its colours and chiaroscuro". [14]

## ONE WORLD

But this is just talk, the common world coinhabited by a visual field and a physical body still eludes us. Are we to say that it is just an abstract world of 'everything that is the case' in which spatial problems are pushed aside? Or are we imprisoned again in our sensory worlds with bodies and their behaviour just the way these manifest themselves there?

A science addressing itself to perception will want to include in all that is the case those facts that produce what a philosopher has called 'technicolour phenomenology.'[15] Accepting a Representative Theory in which our sensory organs present a model of the world mediated by the brain, it assumes a core of phenomenal findings that correspond with 'unlit' physical facts accessible to measurement. These facts then tell us that we share a physical room. But where, then, we may ask, do *we* get a look in?

Providing the physical conditions that, when confronted with a relevantly equipped neural system, provide it with a vista is not enough. The viewer does not come attached, any more than a film projector in an empty house produces its audience. Suppose we adapt that analogy by introducing the way a play station brings physically recorded light-wave frequencies to phenomenal life. Donning VR-goggles that convert frequencies into a three-dimensional vista with terrain can give you a skiing experience.

The experiential 'surround' according to this analogy would be down to some analogue of a patterned bitmap filed in the brain. The technical term 'raster' has indeed been offered as an appropriate theoretical entity, [16] and a 'televisual' system proposed as model with the advantage that it can explain how perception reveals public objects in spite of the brain's complex mediation of the sensory input. [17]

It leaves much to explain. A raster is composed of minute areas of illumination called pixels. These are physical points and therefore particulate, and it is by 'coming to light' in suitable arrays that they form a picture. Being material, they crave spatial location and we should be able to say where they are. Do we see them? Not usually, and only by inferring their presence. How is it then with perception? There is no 'grain' there to detect. [18] Where would it be located? To light up in the configuration that gives the picture, the grain should be visible. It not being so, the picture's relation to its physical basis must be more like that of a DVD, but that too involves pixels. It seems then that the percept is immaculate in this respect, whatever its causal origins from 'object, light rays, retina, optic nerve, lateral geniculate body, optic radiations and visual cortex'. [19]

There should also be room for the player or television viewer. Does the percept come along with its viewer attached or give it spontaneous but only momentary birth? It is more realistic to suppose that some degree of diachronic selfhood must be presupposed, or if selfhood is still in question, a subject of sorts. But whether involved already in some way in the vista or coming to it as an already constituted subject, if not somehow explained away, the viewer's whereabouts has still to be accounted for.

Either the brain provides the special physical background in mental space on which the vista as perceived depends, or the physical background is in the brain's own space and within the limits of whatever patterning possibilities it contains. We are told that space is not, as once thought, a container but the sum of relations between whatever counts as spatial in the relevant respect. But in whatever way defined, the occupants of physical space will themselves be composed of particles and thus, according to the way they are now understood, have 'inner' spaces of the own, these in turn 'occupied' by ultimate indivisibles: currently quarks and electrons. If we are left with the latter of the two above alternatives, that is to say, with the notion of an immaculate or un-particulate 'display' space, as someone has said, it will be 'genuinely mysterious ... how something made of particles, and which can be looked into with suitable tools and instruments, can have an inside not at all accessible to such tools and instruments, [in other words] how it can have an inside in a sense quite different from that in which having an inside is something it shares, if not with particles properly so-called, then at least with things composed of particles'? [20]

Theories uncritical from a scientific perspective have abounded from history's beginning. Other spaces have been naïvely conceived as Euclidean replicas of our own. It leaves fewer conceptual difficulties in moving from one to the other, whether from Earth to Heaven or from Body to Mind, even if we still want to know from which side the door opens. But just how Euclidean does mental space have to be? The idea of the contents of our experience forming their independent space invites possibilities as intriguing as they appear scandalous. Scientific correctness assumes, as for most of us it is natural to suppose, that phenomenal space, the space of sensation, requires for its persistence the continuing operation of a brain. It is hard to believe that our multi-sensory view of the world could survive without those massively layered neural computations that conjure it from a complex pre-sensory input. But what if the working brain were required only for certain aspects of phenomenal space, for example those causally linked to our present perceptual locations and more generally to that part of our repertoire that we need for getting around: our 'I do' capacity? What about memory, imagination and certain kinds of emotion, even reflection, and the more portable functions of conscious life including quasi-sensory imagery as in dreaming? Could *these* persist without the brain's biological support? More to the point, can I?

Of course not, we say. But suspension of settled belief is always worth a try. It may even be a duty when current beliefs become unquestioned articles of faith. Can we truly believe (as against believe truly) that consciousness as we have it is a pure product of the brain? Or are only those aspects of experience that anchor it to our present situation as in perception and movement necessarily bound to the brain, while others float free?

Some scientists – their minds more open to their own – have nevertheless crossed the threshold. A theory with a respectable pedigree from the seventeenth century and recently relaunched as 'Extended Materialism', allows for matter other than that based on 'energy, protons, electrons, neutrons, etc.' It claims as an empirical possibility that 'a person's collection of sensations, images, thoughts and Self' can be described as a 'material system located in a space of its own linked by ... informational relations to the brain'. This, it is said, might account for out-of-body and near-death experiences and might find room for the age-old notion of an astral body. [21] While the idea that the mind's space should be *im*material takes it out of any current scientific reckoning, the general tenor of neuroscientific research has been to discount mental 'stuff' as a requirement for grasping truths about the mind. In both cases, the response to such claims is to challenge their supporters to provide an alternative to the prevailing paradigm.

That of course takes time, a very long time as we know from the history of science. The *status quo* proceeds under its own momentum until some initially freakish but gradually conceivable all-embracing view is finally seen to take care of the several but still disconnected anomalies that have been left aside. Until then researchers, still basking in the sunlight after their escape from the first-personal prison fabricated by misinterpretations of Descartes's 'methodological doubt', will feel justified in continuing their research into the brain while mind extenders watch over its takeover of the manageable world. When asked 'Where in the world?' is the animation that is my experience of my able body, they can say it is *expressed* but not directly discernible in our behaviour.

However judiciously or recklessly we tread the alternative path, the theoretical possibilities opened by the notion of phenomenal space go further than just extending the range of current theory; they require a shift of perspective. Some may side with Kant and say that rather than deepening our understanding of experience, this is just a way of opting out of the rational search for its *a priori* pre-conditions. Even more so in the face of the later Wittgenstein's warnings that if you cannot say what would satisfy the question 'where?', that question makes no sense.

And yet, yes, so long as I keep my mind off all those books charting the way neuroscience makes the view of myself as a single self-conscious subject look more and more like science fiction, I have no difficulty in *imagining* that this what I am. Prior to immersion in the large literature used to back the belief in a strict connectionism that makes the brain indispensable to any experience, it may even seem obviously true. Do I have to *try* to give myself a sense of not being in my brain? However vivid the impression that I am anchored to my body, there is no correspondingly vivid intuition of my experience being anchored to that particular part of it my brain is occupying. In fact, that I am *not* in my brain is as intuitively clear to me as that I *am* in my body. That I am in my brain is as counter-intuitive as that I am at this moment, as some theorists urge, riding an intersection of phenomenal space coupled, in a way of which I can have only a formal grasp, to a physical space with which I have no direct sensory acquaintance. Each being as odd as the other, there is no good reason to prefer the former except that, as ordinarily understood, I and my brain occupy the same space. Strictly, then, it should be no more illogical to suggest that by adopting the latter I might envisage communicating directly with other space inter-sectors without having to call on my or their biological attachment to the physical universe. I may even be able to communicate with some who are no longer attached.

Over the edge? Of course. The point to keep hold of is that we know very well where our brains are in relation to what is sensed as the body while, in spite of headaches and temporarily blurred vision whose causes we will readily ascribe to the brain, the ache and the blur are to all appearances in no way attached to it. The only time I *literally* feel my brain is when it knocks against the wall of my skull as my un-sprung bicycle hits too sharp a curb.

But what about headaches? Here it can be tempting to say I must be feeling my brain but, if that is true, then there is no reason for denying that my whole phenomenal world is an experience of my brain. The pain of a headache is a sensory part of my body-image and I might claim, oddly but not unrealistically, that what feeling a brain really amount to is having a world. Then I and not you would be notionally putting my finger into my brain and we are back where we started.

There is a misleading sense in which being 'inside' might strike us as literally true of my phenomenal world. That my conscious mind and that body-image are 'in' my body is a way of talking we acquire from an outside observer's point of view. Think back to the hammock: my being this 'I' emerged from appreciating that from my continuing vantage point I am my animated body. When hindered in its normal motility, whether by paralysis, stiff muscles, numbness, aches, or anything in my physical being that gets in the way of attempted movement on my part, my body holds me to that extent captive. When it prevents me from lifting my arm, I feel confined *by* and to that extent confined *within* my body in a way that some of the tighter minded theologians might identify as the true 'I' and the cannier philosophers as the transcendental 'Ego'.

Generally speaking, the notion of 'inhabiting' one's body is due simply to the fact that my animated body is one you too can see though without access to its first-hand animation, allied to the thought that from your vantage point I too would be unable to see it. Such experience, from a generalized third-person perspective, leaves no option but to identify persons in their visible animation as *containers* of those ephemeral episodes said to compose their streams of consciousness. Conversely, the world 'out there' becomes where we too belong, the world of deeds done, actual prisons frequented, words spoken, written, or sung. If everyone adopted that perspective, methodological behaviourism would be the order of the day, but luckily it is not.

## *IN TOUCH*

We can talk of a 'sensory' visual field as the final event in a sequence of several causes. But even if it is allowed that light accurately reflects objective properties such as the shape, edge, size and even texture of things we see, what we know of them in experience is never more than what we see, hear, taste, smell or feel. Before light waves acquire a phenomenal sheen in the individual consciousness, it is 'out there' in its frequencies but in an availably measurable form. That is the same for all of us but, although our brains are in most essentials similar, those neuronal complexes are no less individually attached than the VR-goggles we put on when operating a play station. There is no neuronal analogue of Hegel's *Geist* or Frege's 'Mind'. There is no Brain in which our individual neural systems 'partake' and whose grip on the world 'out there' 'subsists' for all to enter into. Not only that, those features of the stable surround that correspond to what is 'out there' are themselves only identifiable relatively to a brain of a certain composition and structure. It is a brain exclusively located in a local segment of the Euclidean space to which the world we consciously share is confined, the same world in which alone science too collects its data. These include those causal feedback chains: the fly touches your arm before you see it and you brush it off without looking. Since I cannot share your visual field, any more than you can feel the tickle on my epidermis, that event is unequivocally private. Why not start, then, with the usefully ambiguous notion of a space in which 'private' tickles and 'public' insects both belong – a 'mental' space, so long as that word, too, is taken so far to mean no more than that features of the kind discussed above occupy it.

With a similar proviso it is a 'logical' space: that swaying hammock discloses a basic 'here'/'there' structure that opens the way to the more abstract but clearly oppositional 'subject/object' distinction. That in turn morphs easily into the prolific 'subject/predicate' distinction so suited to logic but applicable in the first instance to the identification of objects and a classificatory science. In another context it is turned reflexively upon subjects themselves in the terms of their own and others' ways of describing individual lives. As a logical space it contains characteristics and objects of widely varied kinds, some of them material, some aesthetic, others more cogently 'situational', or even more widely but at the same time individually, 'existential'. It is a space to which the analytical minds of philosophers have been drawn and might on their behalf even be called a 'grammatical 'space. But however else, at any even higher level of reflection, we describe it, it is at the same time both a sensory space and the space in which we live.

Forgetting sceptical doubts prompted by the possibility of two people sharing the same colour vocabulary and showing the same responses but one with the spectrum inverted, and also with provisos about colour-blindness, tunnel-vision, and so on, we can take it that, in essentials, the world and its furniture are presented to each of us in much the same way. Simple sapience – if understood as no more than awareness of what is going on, and initially no more than needed to avoid 'bumping into the furniture' – adds to sentience another kind of illumination: that shared radiance in which, with language, we have access to each other's thoughts and, if with self-understanding and imagination enough to appreciate the contexts in which they occur, indirectly also their feelings. A communal dimension is added to this communicative one that helps us to avoid bumping into *each other*. We reach others more directly not in the reasoned prose of a higher sapience, but through the words they use in various ways to express *themselves*.

Since sentience is the inescapably individual backcloth of all our structured experience, whatever thoughts emerge are equally confined to particular instances of their personal occurrences or reoccurrences. Happily, as both Descartes and Kant guessed, sapience as the structural watermark of sentience is never quite absent, even if it generally remains at a level lower than that of a reflection calling for a reflective 'I think' to be drawn into the analysis. Except in mental breakdown, it is a cheque never left quite blank. Yet, assured as we unthinkingly are that our minds for the most part severally and in all essentials deal with their sensory input in the same way, the world nevertheless presents itself to each of us at any moment in a particular mind's way.

The mentality of space is disclosed introspectively in its plasticity, something that we can also experience in our hammock.

It has stopped swinging and the time has come for some dreamy relaxation, though not forgetting where I am – no sense in dropping off. Look up for a moment and ignore all thought of what lies beneath. What you can see of the trees above may lead you to imagine them being the tops of much taller trees. You may now have a sense of being further from the ground than you like. Literally dropping off is a possibility that can occur and, if it does, the possibility, not the fact, you may then experience that curious sense of radical spatial dislocation called 'vertigo'.

It comes also in a medical version having to do with fluid in the 'vestibular' system necessary for balance. In itself the experience is one of dislocation in space. Things immobile in the visible world can appear to do so. On a Saturday night it can be Glasgow that is 'going round and round', but an acrophobic venturing too near the edge of a precipice will feel drawn towards it with the cliff-edge remaining stable. With the same cliff-edge as stable support, the restless sea below offers no fixed point of reference and can bring you off balance: the aesthetics of the waves becomes an abyss into which you may fall. In that case both subject and object lose their 'foothold', while the actual geometry of physical space remains imperturbably the same. It is not the fact of some measurable distance between your feet, your eyes, and the edge that accounts for the dislocation; the change of perspective is itself enough to confront you with a chasm.

Innumerable other examples available to anyone show that spatial awareness is more malleable than the idea of an unalloyed shared space should lead us to suppose. Our worlds, the spaces to which we are confined, our everyday worlds, can be quite small but expand as well as contract. Take the rather elusive sense of familiarity. We may not realize we have it until we lose it when inhabiting unfamiliar surroundings. It can be lost in other ways too, some having to do with psychosis or depression.

Might not this sense of familiarity be a deep-rooted survival strategy, one that comfortingly clothes that naked part of the world we need to feel is ours, and of which we subconsciously suspect that we are only an itinerant centre? The world that is ours, our more or less 'extended' world, may be anything from a single location to some widely shared way of life. In this sense we can inhabit many worlds. But when comfortably at home in one or more, the sense of familiarity slips into the background and while there, becomes a pillow on which we can rest.

Science should be able to detect its own truth in this thought, but we have no need to wait for that version to tell us that things and places have experiential properties that fail to correlate with measurable parts of a shared space. Latent properties like centrality and familiarity, if they come to mind sufficiently to be honoured with a name at all, are indications or manifestations of the responsiveness of the so-called sensory field to our longer- and shorter-term histories. They are existential contributions to experience. Basically, you can talk of them only in the context of someone within a particular conscious episode.

Such individual supplements are features of all human perceptual experience that is not pathologically drained of them. Why indeed should we ever doubt that the inputs to our visual experience are vastly varied both in kind and direction? Behaviour-supporting functions include complex balance-preserving 'feed-back' processing and locally operative short-term memory functions, all contributing an impressive feel to the otherwise purely formal distinctions we make when identifying our experiences, such as 'now' and 'then', 'up' and 'down', 'right' and 'left', 'before' and 'behind', and even 'north' and 'south. Sensory border-crashing in the case of synaesthesia has long been acknowledged. Science should have no difficulty in accepting an un-gated perceptual surround that lets in intruders from within.

## JUST DOING

The critical Kant is said to have usurped the throne of sapience from the still scholastically challenged Descartes. René's *Cogito ergo sum*, 'I think therefore I am', was supposed to apply through and beyond life, but it really works only for the moment: I *am* so long as I think. But then Descartes supposed we do this all the time when awake or dreaming. Immanuel's more spectral 'I think' lasts longer: experience itself depends on it. Without it there can be no sequence stretching both backwards to the past and forwards to a future, and without these there can be no 'now' for an 'I think' to inhabit or reflect upon. Once there, the sequence implies an 'I think', but of its true ('noumenal') nature we know nothing.

You might think (yes!) that fixing it in this role accomplishes quite a lot. But some philosophers have claimed priority for 'I do'. Action precedes reflection and not *vice versa*. The static stance of reflection so characteristic of philosophy itself, and to which it has long provided a privileged place in the scheme of things, is not where we start. We will look into that. Others have claimed that the self-reference implied in 'I do' is still too reflective: all we need is the doing. Thinking of yourself as engaged in whatever it is you are up to merely gets in the way of the engagement. Adverting to what you are doing occurs only when dealing with hiccups in a primordial fluency of 'on-going' adaptive behaviour. But even these dealings may be tapped from a repertoire of learned routines, some of which may be innate. Comes an unexpected hitch, some quick thinking has to be done, even a word put in. Even here there are repair routines ready to kick in on their own.

With all this just 'going on' we may be disappointed when looking for the 'I'. Does it even have an address? Knock on the door if there is one, but maybe there isn't. A celebrated scientist has prophesied that the self supposedly indicated by 'I' will in general 'turn out to depend on several different processes (as, e.g. "memory" does) and [we will see] that it is largely a construct of our brain/mind'. The message is that we should be especially cautious of phrases like "We (or I) experience ..."'. [22]

An example of 'mindless comportment' or 'egoless, situation-governed comportment' has been offered in the expertise of a basketball player called Larry. [23] When asked about its exercise, he says that he doesn't think about what he does, he passes the ball and only realizes he has done so 'a moment or so later'. From this the conclusion is drawn that it is in general wrong to assume that anything like 'what I'm trying to do is this' underlies our practical responses. Larry's kind of 'egoless' comportment is proposed as the final stage of five from novice to expert, expertise being the result of learning, attention, imitation, and rule-following, and the learning process itself one of a gradual restoration of situational integrity out of an original decomposition into context-free, that is to say generally applicable features which beginners are able to recognize and practice applying rules to. Once the relevant regularities are absorbed, the novice-become-adept is able to deal with the situation without applying rules to recognized features: the situation itself evokes the relevant response.

This has a bearing on neuroscience and other explanatory approaches to human behaviour. Any history of the acquisition of expertise is by way of the use of terms in a language not of science but of the macroscopic situation: the world as we live in it. The primary form of human activity is one of 'on-going coping' in which situational integrity has been restored after first being pulled apart in order to be mastered at first piecemeal and when the pieces have been put together, finally entire. [24]

One polemical thrust of this idea is to avoid something we have already discussed, the idea that experience is itself experienced or remarked on at some higher-level, whether or not itself an experience — something that would lead to an infinite regress of experiences of experiences. But here it is the over-used notion of 'representation' as basic to all essentially human activity that is being opposed. A representation would be some articulate 'idea' in a rational creature's head or mind, in this case in the form of a star basketball player's reflective knowledge of what he is currently doing while engaged in what he does so well.

Historically, the motivation here is clear enough as illustrated in the case of Martin Heidegger. He chose to drop the notion of consciousness because convinced that its Cartesian overtones forced upon us a falsely theoretical and disjointed picture of the relation of the human being to the workaday world. Descartes led us to suppose that the conscious mind is what we know best because it is what we are closest to and, as it were, stares at us not just in the face but inside it too, leaving the world outside something whose presence must be argued for. Skipping over theoretical intermediaries and placing us as close as can be to the reality of lived experience, Heidegger provides an account of our ways of being that ignores whatever theoretical items get in the way of the world we live in.

But think back to Larry. Certainly, there are many things he had better not have in mind as he runs, catches, weaves, passes. Any such clutter would only interfere with his immediate goal which is of course to score one, or a 'basket' or 'point'. In the longer term he is trying to help his team win. He may also be trying to stay in the limelight and keep up payments on an Arizona ranch. Such worries are banished in the here and now of getting past that man in front of him.

There is some strain in saying that, in passing the ball instead of the obstructing opponent, this would be something he only realized that he was doing 'a moment or so' later. Is there not an ego-presence of an un-reflective nature that, although not just then in a position to reel off a hierarchy of immediate or ulterior aims, is peripherally aware of the point of its present engagement? If it was really only a moment later that Larry realized where he was, for example, or was trying to score another point, implying he didn't know at the time, might we not begin to worry about his state of mind?

Rather than dispensing with the 'I' just because we assume it can only be a kind of voyeur of current content, is the 'I' not more plausibly seen as somehow inhabiting the content? The self in action is not like someone with non-exclusive ownership to a house, retaining the same identity when moving to another so that another owner can move into the same house with its contents having no inherent tie with either. To see the 'point' of what he does is surely at least peripheral if not more centrally inherent to Larry's 'immediate 'observation that he can't get past this man and so must throw the ball to that better placed team-mate. And why deconstruct the sequential nature of experience into a series of tickertape 'now's' looking for an 'I', when the more obvious task is to describe the sequencing itself?

This of course must be done not from the point of view of an observer with no knowledge of basketball, or even sport, as if this was the way to mirror what goes on in Larry's mind, but from Larry's own rapidly changing but integrated perspective. He, of course, as an expert will not pause to reflect on what to do next, but why should the 'I' be thought to go the way of reflection? Is its claim to be present dependent on only being that of a reporter of, or commentator on, what is going on?

To whatever extent pauses in a continuing stream of unfolding experience may be due to interruptions calling for repair and inducing reflection, such reflection itself is not a matter of going upstairs to peer down into an operation going on below, it is itself part of the flow. Against Kant's 'I think' as a formal attachment to all our experience, what experience itself tells us is that no continuing commentary protocols an under-the-table scanning operation that explains how we pull out the right picture or find the right words from some mental archive catalogued according to our presently activated discriminating abilities. Any such ability is already activated in the experience.

A perspective getting us closer may be provided by the phenomenon of knowing 'how to go on'. [25] It is an ability manifested not only in active physical routines like basketball but also in the use of sentences, knowing where a given sentence is going and being disposed in some not purely behavioural way to see this and not that as the way to go, as against seeing *that* it is the way. It is an ability to recognize mistakes in the very making of them. More particularly, it manifests itself in our being able when asked and able to pause, to say what we are up to by giving an answer in terms of a hierarchy of longer-terms goals of diminishing relevance to what expedience says must be immediately 'in mind'. The 'meaning' of the current activity can be said to be contained 'serially' in the activity itself, not as something to be inferred in a moment of reflection by the player, or by some stray bystander unacquainted with the 'rules of our game'.

## ANYONE AT HOME?

It has long been recognized that the 'now' of an experience relating towards a future from a past is not a succession of stop-go moments as measured by a ticking clock. The present 'moment' merges with a fading past into a future with its foot already in the door. It has been labelled the 'specious present', so called to distinguish the duration of a 'now' as we experience it from the instantaneous flash of a strictly timed moment of consciousness. For William James it lasted about twelve seconds, though others have suggested something nearer five. For James it was 'the original paragon and prototype of all conceived times ... the short duration of which we are immediately and incessantly sensible'. [26]

> Any conscious episode will normally include not only what is focally before the mind (the bus I am running to catch or the lack of physical form which makes it problematic as to whether I'm going to catch it) but also the immediate past (e.g., my already having started to run) and the salient future (what will happen if I miss the bus) with which the present activity is intrinsically connected. [27]

No reflection is needed here, but if given time to think back on what I have been doing, for instance observing something in nature, I can put words to hidden inferences already virtually present in my conscious mind That what I see is green implies that it is seen, and to that, as hinted earlier, can be added being seen means that it is seen *by me*. [28] Neither implication takes centre stage in the conscious mind, but that they *can* do so implies latency in a structure already inherent in the experience.

Apart from being shared by a more or less uniform sentient system common to all who are not in some relevant way impaired, and as the hammock example shows, our sensory input is siphoned through a logical structure and amenable to whatever natural language may supervene. In this context it is not the *word* that we find at the beginning, but a skeletal *logic*.

Certainly, the degree of structure to be found 'in the beginning' is primitive in relation to the requirements of philosophical analysis and scientific theorizing. These are merely basic distinctions as that between what stays put (the trees overhead) and what does not (the swinging hammock or myself). 'Me' and 'I', passive and active, denote a vantage point that changes against stable backgrounds and whose passage through time and space is to a greater or less degree remarked from that mobile vantage point. The ability of this mobile pivot to note and come back to parts of the background outside and in itself – the (grammatical) subject/predicate distinction – is by transference a derivative of that subject ('I') object (it) distinction. It is our basic equipment and all that need be presupposed, whatever the basic equipment itself presupposes in respect of time, space etc. From here on we can classify, construct theory, predict outcomes and reconstruct a universe that is, as has usefully been said, a '[set] of interrelated facts'. [29]

We are reminded that consciousness has evolved to help us around, not to let us in on how it does that.

Knowing *how* it is done is not the same as knowing *what* is done or what (or who) is responsible for doing it. To suppose that whatever might be said from the conscious agent's point of view has no direct relevance, and to look for the answer in the detail and basic architecture of the brain, is diversionary and unduly straitlaced. Does it even *matter* to the agent how it is done? Well, yes, if you think there is no need to go into the background psychology and sociology to know what is 'really' going on. But ask yourself whether microphysics or a close study of neural activity and its hierarchies can tell us why, as distinct from how, a particular location on a turning wheel occupies the position it does? Can the laws of microphysics play anything but a supporting role in the causal explanation of the rolling of a wheel on a cart taking fresh vegetables to market?

Typical statements of a purely neurobiological explanation of human behaviour build from below and aspire to explain the use of language and the ability to conceptualize implicit in the situation of a being advanced enough to be taking wares to a market. But when it comes to language we are given only a promissory note. A typical example notes an evolutionary multi-level build-up in which levels of organization reach a level high enough for states in a nervous system to 'represent or model the world'. Some properties, those at the cellular and synaptic level – as with those of ink in relation to a meaningful sentence – although contributory remain 'invisible' at that explanatory level. Since 'nervous systems selectively represent information a species needs', the precise nature of the world model too is level-dependent: '[n]ervous systems are programmed to certain selected features through experience by encountering examples and generalizing'. Once cognitive neuroscience grasps these latter processes, it will become clear that the 'aboutness' and 'meaningfulness' of a representational state is not a 'spooky relation' but a 'neurobiological' one. When provided, the understanding will be in the shape of a theory of how language is both learned and represented by 'our sort of nervous system'. [30]

There is an archaeological strain to this. To 'explain' the still unexplained icing on the cake (for instance understanding a sentence) we need to reach as far back as the molecules that make up the crumbs. But the explanation if we had it would tell us only what a use of language presupposes. It would get us no nearer explaining the exact location at a particular moment of a place on the rim of a turning wheel on the way to a market. Even if aboutness and meaning are the icing, there is still their use to be accounted for. No cake without crumbs, sure enough, but crumbs never made a cake.

From its 'latest best' perspective evolutionary theory suggests we look at it from the other end, so that what we really want to know are the peculiar properties of a behavioural organism like ours for which the more elemental levels of un-organization and organization belong to a distant past and have been long superseded by what we might call 'control from the top'. We, like the farmer on the way to market, feel we are doing something to our own or someone else's benefit. The sense of 'doing' rather than being done to is part of everyday life. In this respect we all know what it is to have the feeling of what philosophers call agency or what William James calls the 'experience of activity'. Of course, the mere feeling does not let you infer the fact, any more than the sense we have of the sun's going down informs us that this is what actually occurs; certain facts behind our backs tell us it does not do that and explain furthermore how the illusion occurs. So, we could just as legitimately claim that what causes our actions are, for example, nerve processes. For these, too, as James points out, can cause the feeling of activity just as much as they cause the movement. But in his typically open-minded way James points out that there is also something to be said against this. Suppose we take seriously the empiricist thought that the contents of all our main concepts are derived in the first instance from experience. Then:

[a] philosophy of pure experience can consider the real causation as no other *nature* of [a] thing than that which even in our most erroneous experience appears to be at work. Exactly what appears is what we *mean* by working, though we may come later to learn that working was not exactly *there*. Sustaining, persevering, striving, paying with effort as we go, hanging on, and finally achieving our intention – this *is* action, this *is* effectuation in the only shape in which, by a pure experience-philosophy, the whereabouts of it anywhere can be discussed. Here is creation in its first intention, here is causality at work. To treat this offhand as the bare illusory surface of a world whose real causality is an unimaginable ontological principle hidden in the cubic deeps is, for the more empirical way of thinking, only animism in another shape. You explain your given fact by your 'principle', but the principle itself turns out to be nothing but a previous little spiritual copy of the fact. Away from that one

and only kind of fact your mind, considering causality, can never get. I conclude, then, that real effectual causation as an ultimate nature, as a 'category', if you like, of reality, is *just what we feel it to be*, just that kind of conjunction which our own activity-series reveals. [31]

There is general agreement that physics wherever it happens to be involved has to be working in its rigid, rock-solid fashion. But it won't tell us why a molecule on the wheel occupies just that position at that moment of time in the universe of interrelated facts. Why? Because, when applied to any actual situation, what neat thinkers call *ceteris paribus* clauses come into effect, that is to say, interfering exceptions due to the co-application of other 'strict' laws that supervene at ever higher levels of organization. True, the wagoner may still have much to learn about the place of markets in the social economy, and how slips of paper have become exchangeable for goods, and true also that this knowledge has to come from a hard third-person 'look' into the dynamics of interpersonal behaviour, and this in turn from an inherited understanding of human psychology, which may then take us to neurophysiology, molecular biology and the physical basis of human dispositions. The *limits* of possible behaviour may even be charted at that lowest *sine qua non* level. But in order to explain actual behaviour we need a phenomenal world seen within the perceptual and the conceptual orbit of the agent. What, for example, if the actual position of that part of the wheel at a particular moment is due to a rain shower that persuaded the wagoner to spend some time in a tavern?

Yes, the agent. That implies activity and in some sense choice and the elusive notion of freedom.

Freedom from what? In the first instance from rigid levels of the physical basis of human behaviour. But does that have to be proved? Or, to put the onus on those who assume there is no such freedom, is there any incontrovertible argument (or conclusion) from which it follows that psychological phenomena *never* have their *own* causal interrelationships and do *not* behave in the same rigorously deterministic way? Is it not rather that those who think otherwise are stuck in a way of thinking in which matter is itself naïvely understood on the model of things that get in our way, as when Dr Johnson sought to 'refute' Bishop Berkeley's 'to be is to be seen [*esse est percipi*]' by kicking a stone?

Wittgenstein put it more delicately: 'The] prejudice in favour of psychological parallelism is a fruit of primitive interpretations of our concepts ... [f]or if one allows a causality between psychological phenomena which is not mediated physiologically, one thinks one is professing belief in a gaseous mental entity'. [32] 'Why should there not be', he asks, 'a psychological regularity to which *no* physiological regularity corresponds?'

Yes, why not? Although total irregularity or incongruence is not to be expected, writing off any local instance as an empirical possibility involving a 'spooky relation' would be a stifling bureaucratic move that belies any belief in a genuinely inquisitive science. If the 'primitive' idea is the assumption that physical interrelations systematically cause their mental counterparts, then this, too, is surely a prejudice overdue for abandonment.

The same can be said for the tsunami of current theory that deprives us of the notion of activity. Freedom and activity are a related pair, and arguments against overblown notions of freewill take that of agency with them. But freedom as a component in activity is still a far from fully explored or analysed notion. The sketch given above for a bottom-up explanation of our ability to conceptualize and converse spoke of higher levels of the nervous system representing or modelling the world, albeit in species-specific editions of the world. But one of the properties that would need to be included in that promissory note about a theory explaining the use of language is that of *self*-representation. The best excuse for talking of top control is to be able to say that the organism has a grasp of itself as a whole in an environment in which its options are evident. To arrive there (or here) we need a functional link between a conceptual capacity and the human ability to form an idea of itself in the macro-level terms of a Jamesian everyday world with its emphasis on experience as where our ideas of activity and causation belong. It would be nice if we could show that what accompanies the concepts and 'language-dependent' meaning that is needed for an articulate conceptual scheme to be developed, is the ability of the concept-equipped being to represent itself in different lights, situations or worlds. From there we can proceed to see how such a being is able to explore alternatives in thought and to redirect its own predispositions, and to adjust the mental economy that governs the kinds of choice it currently makes. It is in such terms, balanced by what is due to drives beneath the level of consciousness but which are nevertheless to be described in ways derived from the conscious life, that we can again tackle the question of freedom dealt with all too simplistically in philosophy's past.

Any life with aims of achievement or avoidance is filled with reminders of what we should be doing given the time and opportunity. In that and all other relevant respects, minds – the successive contents of their conscious states – are full of such promptings, feelings of what counts for self-esteem, disgrace, applause, fear and hope. What keeps 'me' on track while I am perpetually changing transactions with the immediate environment, whether the track is across a street and 'I' have to look closely about 'me', or some conundrum in mathematics that is troubling 'me', or a word missing in the fourth line of a poem and 'I' am only gazing unfocusedly into space, is some necessarily fluctuating but always virtually present hierarchy of purposes and projects at work.

Whatever depths consciousness plumbs, at the brain it hits bottom. Or in the metaphor of a room at the top, this is the floor beyond which *everything* remains theoretically invisible. If you want to look into the brain, you must exit your first-person stance and move into the third-person world of science.

That might be misleading. You can of course begin out there (or here) and manage to model intelligence in terms wholly intelligible from within that perspective. You will then be left with consciousness now no longer the 'big one' waiting endlessly to be solved but still having to explain it away or look around from something harmless for it to do. There it is, perching awkwardly on the top of a computational or neurobiological mind already working well enough without it. But the whole point of giving consciousness greater due is to suggest, at the same time, that the structure of the brain is such as to enable it to have that greater due, even if an exploration of the brain itself will not explain how we have it or, at best, tells how it lets us have it.

We read that 'aboutness' and 'language-dependent representation' were to be explained by rising to the required level of multi-layered neuronal activity. Another model has been offered in which the evolution of the brain is that of an organ generating ever higher-levels of arousal, culminating in the highly flexible kind of alertness allowed by conceptually organized performance. Like the huge eye of the falcon that allows it to focus a prey at three kilometres and takes up a large part of the brain, our large brains with comparatively much smaller eyes provide a reach over another kind of distance, that felt gap between subject and object that is the basis of all talk of 'aboutness' or 'intentionality'. In their development brain and consciousness go hand in hand (rather than hand in glove). A 'logical-mathematical interpretation of the relationships between consciousness and brain is possible only if their "isomorphism" is admitted'. Yes, but 'inventive and creative activity (which is the activity not of robots and computers but of the brain which constructed them, cannot be reduced to a servomechanism'. [33] AI-modelling is something our brains can do but only by virtue of not conforming to AI-models. Curiously, those models of human intelligence that dispense with consciousness assume that the brain as a biological result of evolution gets in the way. By professional standards it is a rather poor computer, and those who try to model the human mind in this way must resort to 'fuzzy' logics and programs that let in enough 'noise' to measure up (or down) to our everyday standard.

Why, though, seek to model the structure of the human mind by picking out one form of human intelligence and a very specialized form at that, namely the ability to follow strict logical rules? It is far too inflexible a form to capture the features essential to a system that can respond to a complex and ever-changing environment and leaves the modeller with the irrational task of doing justice to the flexibility and apparent irrationality of our actual performance. We should be looking for other models and structures out of which the computational speciality can indeed emerge, but which are not based on and necessarily lack the special features of that particular ability.

In real life, what really clicks for us might be found in the random thoughts of someone lazing in a hammock with no attempt at sustained thinking. But that too is a special kind of situation. Suppose instead that we take a situation that calls for a more concentrated focus: the ordinary town dweller's need to cross a busy street?

Trying my hand at some stream-of-consciousness writing, I might represent my character's stream like this: 'Now's the moment! Quick, before that bus! That's it! Here's the half-way island, safe so far. Should have fastened that shoelace. Catch some breath! Nothing on the right? No, idiot, this is the UK. Clear on the left. Easy does it. Don't trip on the curb. There, I've made it. Thank God. Now over there to the Post Office. Still got that packet? Yes, there it is.'

As in basketball, normal actions *un*guided by rules of play consist of several auxiliary sub-actions, or if you like, a given action, one you can recognize in another, is made up of several longer-term goals. This one's aim is the post office on the other side of the street. But that can be described as yet another auxiliary action, making a deadline, and that yet another, getting that interview, and still further, the job, and the sequence before it runs into the sand may be filled out with yet more, keeping the family, earning a pension . . . and further or deeper still, keeping the mind off those questions for which religion is supposed to provide not always very attractive answers.

Given this prolixity, as against the claim that there is no one at home, it can rightly be said that no one thing is 'being done'. But equally, when we ask someone what they are doing, they will not recite such a sequence or even, just then, bring to mind its longer-term items and some never — psychiatric help may even be required. But in general, the reason for not bringing even closely ulterior goals to mind is that the answer you require of the agent is related to what they are seen to be doing at that moment when no quick answer comes to mind. 'What do you think you're doing?' might on occasion be asked of someone taking what seems an unusual step, and the answer calls for explanation by some goal not obvious to an observer. But asking 'What have you in mind?' presumes that the questioner is not expecting an answer like 'crossing the street', which is too obvious, but something that makes sense of doing so, there and then, with so much rush-hour traffic: 'trying to get to the post office before it closes'. If asked again 'Is it all that important?' 'Yes', you say, 'it's that job'. As you cross a busy street you may just now be concerned not with getting to the other side: that sports car doesn't look as though it's going to stop. In any conscious activity no single accompanying state of mind counts as my knowledge of what it is I am doing or corresponds to what I will say if asked.

So, what about the *words* put into our street crosser's mind? They are of course one way in which a writer might convey what was going on in the pedestrian's mind. But only exceptionally would someone crossing a street actually mouth these words or mutter them under their breath perhaps to help concentration. Overheard, it might sound like public access to the actual performance and, as noted, some theories of the self-conscious mind have claimed a role for such a commentary: a part of my mind is constantly looking at what I am actively 'about' and it is from the information available to this surveillance faculty that the street crosser is able to spout the words given above.

If spoken at all, whether aloud or in an undertone, we may suppose the words to emerge from a speech-centre, which for want of a better alternative we locate in the brain. The implication here is that thoughts emerge as prefabricated units, this being no doubt a useful corrective to premature assumptions about the originating powers of a pre-established 'I' patching sentences together out of separate words before delivering them. We are slaves to our natural languages or others that we master. Only in exceptional cases do we piece our sentences carefully together, as for instance I am doing now. Their deep structure escapes us and thereby their possible logical relation to the way we find it natural to describe what we experience in the way we experience it. Sometimes, as earlier suggested, speech-centres themselves are spoken of as if the words issuing from them were related to the performance in no more intimate a way than a government communiqué issued to the press. If, as it is said, what goes on behind the scenes in this case is a 'massively parallel' processing of countless pieces of 'information', far from being an even severely edited account of what 'goes on' in the brain, the linear form of any commentary precludes it from providing information at all about 'what actually goes on'. All languages are then foreign.

Any record of the conscious contents of a person engaged in even the most focused activity, it has been suggested, would be only 'a variegated jumble of images, decisions, hunches, reminders and so forth...'. [34] But would a neurological explanation tell the true story of what happened when Alan Turing (for it is he whose mind those words were notionally describing) was trying to 'distil the mathematical essence: the bare-bones, minimal sequence of operations that could accomplish the goals he accomplished in the florid and meandering activities of his conscious mind'? [35]

The everyday activity of crossing a street is in some sense obviously mental. It involves sensation, maybe quick thinking and some kind of plan. A popular way of talking might go like this. As I cross the street, many hardwired routines come into play. Mostly they can be left to themselves, like tying your shoelaces or necktie while talking to someone. Indeed, stopping to think how to tie a bow can actually stymie the routine and prevent the performance. Novelty, of course, requires correction. Visitors to Britain from the Continent must adjust to a different leftright rule, and when crossing an unfamiliar street, one should perhaps have some experience of the prevailing speed patterns in the relevant built-up area. But even if speeds can vary, traffic generally sticks to the road and comes in a uniform direction either side of a streetdivider if there is one. Speed differences can be tagged to different sizes and types of vehicle, as also braking distances. All this can be routine 'knowledge'. In its own hierarchy the information relevant to what I am trying to do can occur at a high enough level to be conscious, but the 'input' required to sustain the routines required by the particular performance can descend to 'protopathic' levels over whose routines I would never need to exercise control – they just are there – and for which in any case we have no ordinary words. What I might say I am doing merely skims the surface, indeed only a part of an inherently slippery surface. What comes into conscious focus is too dependent on what goes on out there to be used in some explanation of what I am up to.

And yet, again, the simple linearity of an announcement I make of what I am doing typically masks a passing system of multi-level implication framed by a specific purpose, which makes sense of – and in some way 'informs' – any current means I mention unless there is a mental deficit of some kind. The means, too, are prone to possible replacement as relevant phenomena in the environment catch my eye or ear, their relevance determined by and cast into relevant routines through past experience. In crossing the street, some will say that anything I might call my conscious self is engaged merely as an operative part of a behavioural system: it 'kicks in' when revision is called for. These revisions are made *ad hoc*, certain provisos come to mind, even some taking stock before continuing, perhaps not stepping off the curb at all: that truck some distance away on the left seems to be going rather fast and, with the braking distance required for such a vehicle in mind, I stay put. I may even turn back. But that, in turn, will depend on whether I am taking the air or on an important errand.

When all that is said, there is no getting away from the obvious fact that in anything we do, even if what we may provisionally call the 'subject pole' is focused on salient aspects of an 'object pole', this 'behavioural system' is also a 'project' system that is meeting a changing world in which its projects at any moment can be realized or frustrated. The fact applies equally to those theorists of mind who look at mental phenomena from 'outside'. There is a sense in which if any operation at all is going to be successful, drafting an essay, composing a poem, extracting DNA, solving a mathematical problem, or even just going for a walk, it is in terms of some shorter or longer-term goals or aspirations of which this can be seen as a part. Actions are subject to scales of preferences that, even if we are only rather feebly aware of them, form our active *curricula vitae*. The stock we take in and of a situation draws on our own dispositional trademarks, you could call it personal background. The more relevant stock I can take or options I have at my finger-tips, the more effectively engaged my current comportment and correspondingly less at the beck and call of 'my' neurons. The more reason, accordingly, to say that here we have a form of self-knowledge in practice in which this 'I' is essentially engaged. Looking at the rags and refuse of a stream of consciousness more closely, you should find not only threads but among these even stories, signs of unity of the self fairly well within the contents of consciousness.

This someone at home is not confined to an empty attic and looking through a hole in the floor, or several floors, in the direction of what you need to know to grasp what 'really goes on'. Looking long enough into the highest floor's jumble of contents, you should find some degree of residency up aloft. You may in some cases even find enough there to exchange the attic for a bungalow, one that has no need of a cellar except perhaps for less transparent matters that may call for some probing in the cellar by a psychiatrist.

## COMING UP WITH SOMETHING

Yet let's face it, you will say. To whatever degree the results of Alan Turing's mental agonizing might be applied to the actual workings of his mind, the conscious comings and goings come nowhere close to what was going on in terms of arriving at his conclusions. At best what was manifest in Turing's consciousness were ill-assorted and disorganized mental grunts and groans, or whatever hunches and reminders opportunely or not 'came to mind', none of which gets anywhere near, and the whole of which gets nowhere near what he was actually doing, namely approaching the specification of that abstract system (the Universal Turing Machine) which is able to compute what a computer of any internal design can compute. [36]

How much, then, does innovative or creative thought of any kind, whether science, poetry or just a good idea, depend on phenomenal association?

A reasonable guess is quite a lot. Who is to say it isn't the sight of a branch or the shape of a twig that puts a genius on track as he wanders through a wood or provides the long sought-after metaphor for an unfinished stanza. Finding yourself looking at an empty page and standing at the edge of a pavement about to cross a busy street are clearly quite different. But both are complex situations where how to go on is not already embedded in the action. We can begin with the latter, it being more typical of what most people have to contend with.

For an able body enculturated at home, unlike some visiting tourist used to a more pastoral setting, the expectations and hazards here will be second nature. Quick thinking will be necessary but nothing new has to be learnt – no acculturation, no innovation. In either case, conceptual adaptation is a process in which the organism-in-action faces a reality conceived in the schemes that inform its current environmental engagement. And because reality typically transcends the scheme and the moves dictated by the project, rigidity would in any case be disastrous. Conceptual systems are not rigid; nor are the concepts themselves that form them, or the rules of their use. In other words, if flexibility were not a feature of the rules rather than in any relevant sense an infringement of them, we would not be here. An answer to the admittedly loaded question 'What is consciousness good for?' could be that at some level of its own, or in several levels in combination, consciousness is the flexible medium in which regularity and randomness meet and novelty can rise to the practical occasion. How then are we to describe this flexibility?

'Is a soul greater than the hum of its parts?' That's nice, it's as inventive as the title of the book you will find it in, *The Mind's I*, [37]encapsulating in a pun as it does the whole question of the mind's image of itself. In those three short words we read that the idea of any 'I' that the mind comes up with is no more than that, simply an idea, and a bad one at that. Is it perhaps that besides being inventive, amusing and pithily expressive, the punning style is also felt to be necessary in promoting the cognitivist's case? Are our traditional beliefs so entrenched that something more than argument, some elbow nudging, a friendly push or some rhetorical pumping, are needed to shake disbelievers out of their egocentric habits?

Since we may assume that inventiveness is the mark if not a monopoly of human intelligence, what our source has to say on this aspect, illustrated so well in the hum of his own parts, is much to the issue. He has proposed that the way in which the characteristic 'fluidity' that enters into the more predictable structures of human intelligence can best be explained by a notion of 'statistical emergence': 'Intelligent behaviour, especially the fluid behaviour of concepts, can be likened to the regular macroscopic behaviour of a physical fluid, and the microscopic substrate of intelligent behaviour can be likened to the molecular-level randomness that, through the regularity of statistics, gives rise to physical fluidity. It is ... thanks to statistical emergence that the roles played by randomness and non-randomness in intelligent behaviour can be reconciled.' [38]

Suppose, however, that innovations are responses to gaps defined at the level of the conceptually configured activity to which some current environment-management belongs. It need not be verbal, it may be purely manipulative, calling on resources of know-how some of which we never knew we had. Whether or not linguistic, or verbalized, innovation is typically a response to breaks in organization, disruptions of rational and also habitual expectation. In literary innovation, by breaking the habits and destroying the routines of the speech centre itself, we can produce the kinds of gaps that attract innovation. The innovator need not be a passive recipient of creative ideas, sitting back and waiting patiently for a statistically regulated off-chance to materialize. The vacuum in which the as yet unknown but hoped for idea emerges can be deliberately created.

Some responses to needs made at the higher functional level, as in certain kinds of art, no doubt require a state of passivity for the 'solution' to emerge, or even just doing something else for a while, an experience we all recognize. Other responses are to the contingencies we face in our everyday activities, the gaps provided by the developing situation and which call for rapid readjustment. In both kinds it seems theoretically naïve to explain fluidity simply as a matter of indeterminism breaking in on algorithmic routines from below, especially if the deficits or imperfections that release the creative energy are identifiable only in the shared phenomenal world.

Still, in allowing that the more multi-layered the process, the greater the statistical chance of novelty, the bottom-up picture does point to something that a less dislocated conception can profitably inherit. That there are levels of consciousness is no secret; consequently, there is no inherent problem in placing the threshold of input into the speech centre nowhere lower than, or somewhere very near, the lowest level of consciousness. The greater the mix of imagery and half-baked ideas that goes into the blender, the more chance there is of coming up with something rewarding at the executive level.

Apart, then, from that power to disrupt and make space for something new to keep us on track, there is this other idea of novelty involving the interaction of several levels in a hierarchy tending to verbalized thought or to 'seeing' what to do. Images, for instance, would be lower than linguistic organization. Old philosophy spoke of an autonomous imagination ready to work night and day but deadened by our daily cares and the need to focus on such necessities as crossing streets safely. One old philosopher, Thomas Hobbes, thought sheer daylight did the same job: conveniently as well as necessarily, it pressed our chaotic and insistent dreams into the background while we got on with the job of life. [39]

Continuously flowing beneath the visible surface there may be lower-level streams of jumbled ideas, fears and hopes, recollections. Like the Joycean stream of consciousness and similar variants as, for example, William Faulkner's, this too is an image, one that the mind produces of itself and its own workings. Saying that it emerged from this latter stream is merely to repeat the image. Where it actually comes from or how to describe this hierarchy, who knows? Can we ever replace simplistic imagery and metaphor with an evidently true account of 'what goes on'?

Maybe not, but an image with some anchoring in common experience that takes account of ways in which creative poets, genius mathematicians, composers, and even the resourceful quick-fixers all of us inherently are, has a better *prima facie* claim to be taken seriously than the analogy of statistical emergence. The fluidity of intelligence is a notion introduced to distinguish open-ended problem solving from those more 'crystallized' forms of intelligence where considerations accounted for are established and steps taken closer to being deduced. [40] 'Fluidity' contrasts with 'viscosity' and suggests the easy flowing movements of a basketball player as opposed to those of exponents of such 'stickier' set-piece forms of sport such as baseball or cricket. In itself, fluid is as regular as can be. If water, then so long as it doesn't turn into either ice or steam, and even if liable to separate and form drops, it remains absolutely regularly fluid, while the intelligence of regulated behaviour lies precisely in its being open at all times to deregulation and re-regulation. Rather than a matter of statistical emergence due to something like molecular randomness below, fluidity is a feature of a level of intelligence to which molecular activity plays a theoretically invisible and only ancillary role.

## THE EYE'S MIND

We assume that consciousness has evolved to help us around but without letting us in on how it does that. Might it not also be the case that our cognitive faculties for the same reason do not let us in on the true nature of the reality they are out to grasp? Getting around is a practical matter: we can measure and sort the furniture of the world enough to avoid bumping into it, or damaging it beyond repair. Our first needs have to do with survival. But we do, once in a while, look up from the feeding trough and wonder 'What is the point of it all'? We may do that despairingly when there is too little food to go around. Why should science not help us here too, not just the food but those questions that arise when our stomachs stop aching?

Consider a possible analogy. After over two thousand words re-searching time in his own experience of it, Marcel Proust describes the retake as a deciphering of a script dictated to him by reality. The bare facts of a life lived stare at us as a log recording the merely factual details of a voyage. We may not care to look at it all, but it is a public record. You can distribute it and share it with others. In a crucial sense, though, even if complete in this way it is still not yours. To make it so, you must 'decipher' what reality has dictated, for as Proust says, 'what we have not clarified by our own effort can never be ours'. [41]

The question someone looking up from that trough can ask is, 'Can, by some special effort of deciphering, the *world* be made ours?' You might say that science has been deciphering the dictates of reality ever since the Greeks and Egyptians and before, as also further east and west. But this doesn't make the point; the analogy requires that the deciphering be a matter of personal appropriation and that is something quite untypical of today's science, engaged as it is in the theory-driven collection of measurable data cleansed of the slightest personal input and interference. Its aim is a unified theory of all that is, this including what causes the theory-fugitive ephemera of what merely passes in the measurer's mind.

Theory also has its history. And Greek Antiquity's *theoria* had its scientific basis too. The word meant 'contemplation'. This was neither navel-gazing nor its opposite: the disengaged view of modern science. But it is worth noting how the removal of the person works in either case. In Greek *theoria* it was the goal or *result*: an intuitive sense of unity that was the intended outcome, something very different from a discipline of detachment designed to eliminate the 'noise' of an individual researcher's input. Allusions to drug-taking are in order and, of course, also to the cultivated sense of cosmic belonging associated with the East, which is recognized to have an influence on Greek thought. Such belonging would be enjoyed in religious rites – the 'mysteries' – in the presence of the *theoroi* who served as goodwill ambassadors and whose 'observing' took the form of overseeing the games and festivals of the various city-states. Incidentally, as a small step in the direction of national co-operation, they also acted as guarantors of peace among the participating states at the time and of safe passage for those attending,

The subject/object relation has, accordingly, its own history too. From the math-minded Pythagoras's music of the spheres to Hegel's reasoned Absolute, the histories of philosophy and science have offered several alternatives. Might the view presented here of an outside world dictated by circumstances to which our own mental organization contributes nothing be the result of a process of the consolidation of the 'I' which is at the same time one of its increasing alienation from the cosmos?

Our cognitive powers are currently conceived as those of a machine-scanner recording a ready-made script. There is no room for a deciphering that makes it 'our own'. Any sense of homecoming in a cosmos 'out there' must be left to a plug-in fideism in which science has no part. It is of course always possible to wonder at the world dictated to us, and to raise questions like Heidegger's, copied by Wittgenstein, 'Why is there something rather than nothing?' The question framed in that way has a theological ring, as if there might be some purpose in there being a cosmos, as that more fastidiously rational thinker Kant was quicker to embrace. He went so far as to say that knowledge of the ultimate nature and point of it all must be denied 'in order to make room for faith'. [42]

From the hearth to the front door or garden fence and to varying degrees beyond, we all know what makes a piece of the world *feel* like home. Hanging pictures on the wall, walking the same streets and exchanging smiles with neighbours can be a start. We are, usually without thinking, 'at home' in some part of the world. But the cosmos? How could we ever feel let alone actually be at home in that?

Philosophers have become specialists in a world of their own specification, a world of organized objects and practices they themselves have devised and with skills only they can appreciate. But what other ground has philosophy ever had to stand on? Looking back to its origins won't help. The history of philosophy is of all those wonderers who have similarly sought to find a platform from which to discern the shape of human fulfilment. For the philosopher, fulfilment is the same as it is for anyone: not the filling in of a space but a clearing of the way back to the only stable platform we have, our own reflective contact with a single world that we know we share, with hopes also held by others even though we do not all hope for the same. That should make us think more carefully about ourselves and more readily about others.

That may be the hope held out by philosophy, but fear of being nowhere was what led to its pursuit. As an escape into thought, or perhaps even a genuine attempt to retrieve reality, it looks in retrospect like a vain attempt to think the way back to home. But whatever first drove people to philosophize, might not this fear have shaped the discipline down the centuries by making *certainty* its ideal? If indeed philosophy is just another expression of that fear, it stands in deep contrast to the form of human fulfilment it aims to vindicate. If diaries can be written to alleviate the pain of grief, may not philosophy be a fantasy flight into those words with which ceaselessly thinking thinkers have tried to put the *unheimlich* behind them?

Positivism tells us to forget the whole thing. Its motivation was partly political: thinkers who thought otherwise were too easily presented as totalitarian. Existentialism leaves it to our individual selves to decorate the blank walls of the universe. In *La Nausée,* his first novel, Sartre portrays the efforts of an unemployed ex-adventurer turned historian but already rootless Antoine Roquentin. He lives in deprived conditions and with only passing human contact. Temporarily resident in the provincial town of Boueville – or 'Mudsville' – he fills his own life by investigating the exploits of an eighteenth-century secret agent. In doing so, his own existence shrinks to a mere point, his own world becomes one that has no room for him, a fact to which he realizes it is quite indifferent. Lacking rhyme or reason, it simply 'is'. [43] In glaring contrast to Roquentin's desolation, a bevy of self-satisfied dignitaries basking in their civic reputations beam down at him from the walls of an art gallery.

With its original title 'Melancholia', the novel was conceived as a case study of mental illness with nausea just another symptom. In the light of what came immediately after, it is clearly an in-life introduction to Existentialism. The parable of one man's nausea reveals the state in which those deprived of the protective self-deceptions of 'bad faith' have what philosophers might call a 'privileged access' to our situation *vis-à-vis* the cosmos.

For Roquentin, 'existence' or the world as he finds it is gluey, slimy, sickly, visceral. Although trees smile when he brightens up at the thought of writing a novel, this only shows how existence takes on values that we give it in the situation. This is our freedom, one that lets you define yourself as free even in captivity. Less paradoxically, the world acquires meaning, but only by having the varying modes of our confrontation projected upon it. Negation, for instance, is constantly hovering at its edges. We are not so much in a world of everything that *is* the case, but one of hope or fear of what might *be* the case

– of all that is *not quite* or *yet* the case, or of what is thankfully not the case. In brief, the phenomenal world is a sounding board reflecting our fears and hopes. With whatever inspiring artwork or graffiti, you decorate the walls of an in-itself world, the walls themselves remain resolutely bare.

Like those extensions of the mind-as-brain that colonize the world with street signs and time-tables, existentialists make it their own by conceiving it as a *carte-blanche* on which to place their own imprint. Both take possession of a small part of the universe in a way that provides purpose, engagement and belonging. No one is there to welcome them from the other side, nor in principle is there any need. So too with science. Although the universe never presents a wall that is blank – or so it is said, since all observation is theory-laden – this does not mean that the outside world reveals its true nature to theoretically innocent observers. It means that all observation is infected by theoretical presuppositions, whether professionally scientific or popularly 'folk-theoretical'. Something is always being added to the datum from the subject side. As in the wave theory of light, scientific theories are strings of technical terms arranged on the subject side to define a general principle that makes the phenomenon intelligible. To suggest that phenomena might be shining a light on themselves will invite, if not hollow laughter, a polite smile.

Yet some investigators have taken it seriously. Although his conclusions are easily derided for their scientifically incorrect presentation, Goethe's own observations on light and colour, on minerals and skeletal and plant morphology were nevertheless meticulously recorded. Schopenhauer, Gödel, von Helmholtz, and Wittgenstein were more than intrigued. Even Heisenberg saw the positive influence of Goethe's science though noting that victory in the case of the spectrum and colour had been conceded to Isaac Newton.[44]

Nature, even to an inveterate observer of its detail, does not deliver its secrets of itself. It must first stimulate some idea in the naturalist's mind, one that further observation may support, unless earlier observations help to generate it in a 'eureka' moment like that sought by Goethe himself in a Palermo garden: 'Here, where, instead of being grown in pots or under glass as they are with us, plants are allowed to grow freely in the open fresh air and fulfil their natural destiny, they become more intelligible'. He was on the lookout for the Primal Plant: 'There certainly must be one. Otherwise, how could I recognize that this or that form was a plant if all were not built upon the same basic model?'[45]

# THE ORTHOGRADE POSTURE

Whether found *in* Nature or applied *to* it, some contribution from the mind is needed to make the phenomena intelligible. Blank gazing gets you nowhere. Still, being able to gaze has some obvious advantages. A not at first obvious one is that it requires distance. Although I may gaze at moving clouds between the tree tops while lying in a hammock, typical gazing involves standing up. It also helps to stand back as when retreating far enough from a large billboard to see a 'meaningless' expanse of colour as a picture.

Although spending half of our lives supine, that is to say, flat on our backs, the distance provided by the ability to stand upright is endemic to human experience. It is something that 'we' have achieved over an unimaginably long haul and only in its course has the world we know gradually formed. It is not the world we have got up from. Supposing otherwise is to fall into an even cruder version of the naïve realism in which we generally and quite naturally assume that what we perceive persists as perceived with no one present to perceive it. This second-level naïveté would take what we perceive to be as we perceive it even to creatures that do not enjoy the distance created by the upright stance.

This stance invites various characterizations besides just letting things come into view. The individual's own coming into view can also be seen in its light:

> Only when our 'op-position' towards the ground has been firmly established do we gain that distance which allows objects to appear in their own structure and *gestalt*; then, incorporated into this universally valid order, we are first enabled to meet others and to communicate with them as partners. [46]

The mist-clearing that provides the beginnings of an objective world also 'constructs' the gazer as an individual, making communication and also partnership possible but necessary. The author's concern here is with the psychiatric implications of a relapse that erases the sense of being one separate self among others. As a virtual practising behaviourist, the psychiatric patient loses 'sight' of others as distinct centres of experience whose utterances and actions issue from a life that is being lived by another subject. But that situation is not a monopoly of the psychiatric patient. The words 'Yes, of course I know there are others!' slip out so easily and *pro forma* they say that there are others like myself, 'subjects of experience' as our teachers used to call them. And the basic ethical insight is indeed that those we meet in relevantly ethical circumstances are 'just like us' in respect of what we fundamentally experience in ourselves. But the insight is one that waxes and wanes between acquiescence to a mere form of words and a genuine sense of there being others like us in the way that we are sensible of being ourselves. One may say a little cynically that it is a sense we have when it suits us but are liable to lose in a twinkling when the opportunity offers. Less cynically, there is a universal temptation to do so that requires ethical resistance whether institutional or personal. The upright stance, or 'orthograde posture' as it is called to distinguish us from other creatures who can walk erect on two legs as, for example, those waddling penguins, is the break with nature's innocence. We might envy those squadrons of birds wheeling about in close formation as they find their bearings for a long flight over continents and oceans as the seasons dictate. They may leave us with a feeling that Dame Evolution has left us with a gaping need for something that, with our various backgrounds and abilities and urge to survive, can bind us similarly together.

What can strike us as quite significant about those echelons of birds is that there are no selves up there. Their purposive togetherness is not a result of intercommunicative planning by representative committees, nor have they any form of communication with which we in our 'op-positional' singularities are familiar. It seems that after an initial but quite short stage of growth these feathered bipedal beings get it all together quite naturally. Does that mean that, by standing on what evolution tells us were once our hind legs, and to pay for this world-scanning, self-scrutinizing perspective from whose 'subject' pole the world appears as an outside environment, we, the human species as one among others, are worse off for having lost something?

The question is pivotal as to whether finding an effective way of gathering in the 'social' slack, say by becoming selves, even our own selves, is to be understood as a repair operation or an opportunity to go one better than the birds.

Under theological tutelage, the upright stance has been interpreted as just such a species-unique opportunity. In some versions it is a chance to appreciate the wonders of creation. A counterview more relevant to the situation today would be that, in spreading diversity, the mechanisms of natural selection have generated such survival-inimical and nature-destroying social vices as short term-greed, elbowing, ignorance and jealousy.

Probably most of us believe that we are better off than the birds because ethics and a working morality are also an achievement made possible by the upright stance. But here again there is a choice. A pragmatic line with ethics and morality sees its constraints in a utilitarian light, cooperative activity being essential to survival. Psychologically, also in a pragmatic sense, identities and controlled gregariousness (whether exclusionary identities or in some ideal form of a universal 'we') form a buffer against existential insecurity and even homelessness. In that quandary some see a need to gain respect by receiving it from others, these then having to be recognized as equals if their respect is to have the required effect. That would be a typically humanist explanation, as against one like Immanuel Kant's. For Kant, ethics is founded on respect for the Moral Law, and that is laid down by God. The Word is in that case with Him, if only by proxy and, for us, an ideal.

## *LOGOS*

The word translated 'word' in St. John is the Greek 'logos'. It has several meanings but one stems from 'lego' or its infinitive 'legein' in the sense of to 'lay in order' or 'arrange'. *Logos* for both ancient Greece and our John of the Gospel is divine reason as manifested in the order and shape of the cosmos, in contrast to the formless matter of chaos. Not just words, not even just one word, but structure is surely what the Gospel talks about when itself beginning with 'In the beginning was the word' and going on memorably to say that the word was with God and that the word 'was' God.

Does this mean that the structure is a demonstration not only of divine reason but of divinity itself? Or are the two in some way the same? We can perhaps see it in this way: by 'structure' (in its universal validity in a strong sense) is meant an ideal of *universal* partnership: a world in which universal mutual respect would count as divine in itself. But so long as the ideal remains unrealized, this universal *gestalt* is still 'with God'.

Some brief comments on this manner of speech with regard to the 'beginning' being now in order, we can start again with Immanuel Kant. Together with the upright stance and enabled by it, but perhaps more intimately connected, is the placement of an automotive subject pole in a 'now' with a future to anticipate and a past to look back to. The subject is, to itself, the centre of its world in the sense of being surrounded by things including others recognized as centres of theirs – a world which we realize that we to a great extent share. Our phenomenal worlds have a structure dependent on a continuing 'I' (whether or not it 'thinks'), but about this otherwise naked self we know nothing of its ultimate nature. All we can deduce is the ability to synthesize experiences into the categories that give them their structure and universally valid form. Even this is something we have no need to think about: the world appears to us already 'dictated' in the forms of structured experience. Kant, as we recall, tells us that reason must leave room for faith, the latter being what gives us a cosmically dimensioned sense of purpose. The word here still rests with God.

Philosophy after Kant tried to bring us into a more intimate relationship with the cosmos. Hegel presents it as an Absolute to be arrived at in a dialectic, an internal dialogue in which sharp oppositions brought to light by the intellect are resolved in a higher unity, the highest that of being one with the cosmos, the very subject/object opposition itself now dissolved in a unity of both.

This earned Hegel the rebuke from his former student friend Schelling, that although Hegel had provided an intellectual God's-eye view of the cosmos, no provision had been given for the belief that God had actually revealed himself in this light. Schelling, by providing an evolutionary scenario in which God actually does reveal himself in nature and beyond, tried to do better but only by rehearsing the history of religion. The effort in a series of famous lectures in Berlin in 1841, attended by among others

Marx, Engels, Bakunin and Kierkegaard, produced some derision in his audience. As just another recapitulation of a spiritually driven version of evolution that ends in God revealing himself in a personal form, but with no greater power to convince than any other storyteller's, this attempt to take the word from God's hand also failed.

Schelling's critics, Marxist and existentialists in particular, had a different objection. However captivating, Schelling's story was another set of abstractions with no bearing on actual life. It omitted all mention of the economics of living and of the trials of selfhood, each becoming the respective defining theme of those traditions. But what more is there to say? Both Marxists and existentialists have close-focused on the respective deficiencies without taking us not only no further than Kant but not so far. Some will argue that we haven't come even that far. For historical materialists, the word is not with God but in the socio-economic laws which when linked to natural resources determine humankind's future. For existentialists it has been said of Sartre that he emptied God's office only to place us there. The word is with us but it is no longer God's. Among attempts to bring the word to Man are those that claim the noumenal reality that Kant tells us is out of reach is nevertheless available to our understanding and translatable into action, this being where the Word becomes visible.

Panpsychism, on the other hand, in the words of a recent exponent brings the 'noumenal' world only within our *intellectual* grasp, by virtue of that world being conceived as 'innumerable interacting centres of experience or streams of experience including our own consciousness and [those] other consciousnesses, which we normally believe in'. [45] They are all 'contained within one single absolute consciousness', so that '[a]ll finite experiences relate to it in a way somewhat analogous to that in which the individual sensations of any conscious finite individual at a moment belong to his, her or its total state of consciousness'.

Yes, 'its', for animals too are included, not only apes and birds but creatures lower down the scale, even, we assume, as far down as the *infusoria*, those practically invisible aquatic micro-organisms whose response to light waves is said to be minimally like ours, but whose entitlement to the description 'interacting centres of experience' must be taken in a purely organic or impersonal way. Some idea of it conveying a sense of a homecoming in the universe finds expression in the tentative claim that it suggests 'at any rate that human and cosmic history is not simply a false tale told by a non-existent idiot signifying nothing, but is, however slowly, moving towards some extraordinary climax ... at which the last word will be with joy and goodness rather than the suffering and wickedness (though much of the latter must remain an eternal blot on the nature of things.' [48]

If that 'last' word' is the Word that is in the beginning and within reach in the form of joy and goodness, it sounds very like finding us at home in the universe, at any rate more so than making ourselves at home in it. However, the Word will still be available only to those able to put actual words to their happy state, which seems a pity. This interestingly out-of-step philosopher's conclusion is the guarded one that 'metaphysical positions arrived at argumentatively may have significant religious implications for their proponents'. [49]

We must bear in mind that however cosmic in their scope, arguments leading to a metaphysical position are essentially forensic. They are like progressive steps in a brief designed to face down other views. We are, in *other* words, still in the forum. The sentences are just sign-posts, not *functional* clues to a new way of seeing things. [50] What we need is hands-on facts, that is to say first-hand science, a science that relaxes its tight-laced refusal to look 'inside'.

There has been or perhaps still is such a science, or one heralded as such, that tells us that the oppositional situation in which we find ourselves contemplating a world 'out there' has meant a corresponding loss that it is the task of this science to exploit by making it good.

It calls itself a spiritual science. In the absence of any better candidate, there has been a temptation to accept the 'I' that occupies the subject pole as a suitable candidate for possession of a property called 'spirit'. But spirituality in this other tradition is an impersonal property to be discovered in the fact of being an experiencing being. Like the impersonal 'existentials', those categories of being ('care', 'state of mind', 'understanding', 'thrownness', etc.) that Heidegger lists as the structural elements of 'Dasein' (or 'being there'), [51] here a 'purely physical being can have no existence', and to exist at all 'it must have an ether and an astral body, and an ego'. [52] In the long run not just those primitive aquatic organisms, but a stone too is to be understood in this way, these latter aspects belonging to a higher reality from which the stone as we know it in our confinement is an abstraction.

Like natural science, this spiritual version remains in a sense 'impersonal'. Not, however, in order to eliminate the 'noise' of subjective input, for here the 'I' is interested in its own nature beyond being an individual, and in something on the 'I'-side of that oppositional gap that 'rises above the personal'. It is to this higher truth that St. John's *Logos* is now claimed to refer, signifying that the spiritually aware but previously 'mute' and 'imperfect' human once existed in a higher reality without the 'Word'. [53] In this light, the crucifixion of Christ is seen not as atonement for our sins today or to-date but as testifying to the death that 'stands at [the] centre of [life's] becoming ... the death on Golgotha' being its 'true reality'. Humanity itself must outlive a train of dying generations to appropriate the truth of a higher reality within which it has been unreflectively immersed, but to which the development of the upright stance has allowed it to withdraw sufficiently to be able in principle to appropriate the word. [54]

The evolutionary time-scale of this inherently millennial conception in which our deaths pave the way to a spiritual fulfilment in some far-off future, is glaringly open to sceptical doubt. There are also dubious political and dangerous psychological implications to be exploited for reasons to be uncovered by sociologists and psychiatrists. If not just for safety's sake, but also to preserve what we have of democratic society, we can prefer the standard Christian interpretation of the crucifixion as fastening our minds on what we patently still lack in terms of an ideal of universal fellowship.

Such reservations, crucial as they are, do not directly affect the possibility that while the subject/object separation has meant an isolation that erases any memory of some former experience, it at the same time opens the way to a science based on experience that still qualifies as 'empirical'. Even if the evidence is not available to everyone, opening our minds to possibilities of this kind can broaden the mind and pave the way to a better awareness of where we stand.

Recall that opening trio: Empedocles, Plato and Wittgenstein and the different ways in which they took words to express or mirror a world. They form a progression – or regression if you like – from an earlier less individuating consciousness. Might not the aphorisms of Empedocles be the dreamy expressions of a sense of exile from a higher sphere to which he still had a sense of belonging? His poetic words would then be evocations of a half-forgotten past. Soon afterwards came Plato and the awakening of *thought* as a way to recapture that past from a distance, or from inside a cave: ideal forms, or ideas, represent a spiritual sphere only roughly exemplified in actual existence.[53] Now, over fifteen hundred years later, we have Wittgenstein and a world of terrestrial confinement accessible in prose and with a user's label saying that in matters not thus accessible we should hold our tongues – something, if it is also the case, the conditions of whose truth may not be so easily, or similarly, accessed.[54] Not unfittingly, Wittgenstein trained as an engineer in balloons researching an upper atmosphere still within reach.

The terms of any science claiming such things are not 'theoretical' in the way we now think of theory. A language of etheric and astral bodies, for instance, is that of entities of which seers and researchers of the esoteric claim to have first-hand experience by actually being them, and their credentials remain open to doubt and suspicion. Even with exceptions whose inner researches in this area appear to be scrupulous and the result of a life-long commitment, there is the danger that, like Southern Baptists, those taking their versions of the truth on trust have personal motivations for doing so. They reinforce an innate disposition to the closed mind, or, as one might say, a propensity to vulgarize that already suspect Kantian reason for ignorance: that it leaves room for faith, in this case in one's own rectitude.

The same of course applies to those who predict the ability of neuroscience to explain what we already have in the way of intelligence and understanding. Until more brain-searchers follow the example of those few willing to look into their own minds, nothing prevents unschooled observers from looking into theirs. They can test for themselves some claims made on the basis of special experiences, even those that present esoteric conceptions of the human as, for example, that we are composed of four 'members': a physical body, an ether or life body, an astral body and an ego, or that we are not a dualism but an alliterative trinity of mind (wondering), metabolism (willing), and motility (walking). Reflecting on our own dreams lets us test claims about what seems missing there. For instance, how much 'I' is there in dreaming? Enough to engage the 'I think'? Is there room for 'I do' when objects no longer retain their identities? Can you, when dreaming, reflect on what you have just dreamt you were doing or seeing? Are there smells in dreams as well as sounds? Is there enough fore and aft to station a Kantian 'I think' midships in a specious dream present? The uninitiated can of course do little where claims are based on special states of mind but, as argued here, in the face of official dismissals of the importance of what passes in the conscious mind, there is far more of theoretical interest and possible import to note in everyday experience than we are led to expect.

Not that introspection has been ignored. A considerable literature deals not only with the aesthetics of space but also with blind-sight, eidetic imagery, hallucination, the relation between percept and verbalized response, facial recognition, and details such as hallucination outshining normal visual sight. The aim has always been to find corresponding neuronal states, and investigation can show, for instance, that different 'mechanisms' are at work even in saying what you see. The mind's eye is apparently not itself lexically equipped, [57] so that reporting what you see is the product of two operations. The aim in looking for explanations of these is to catalogue the 'underlying' causal chain, but as one neuroscientist has said, introspection can also serve other purposes, in particular that of throwing light on purposiveness itself:

> Normal perception includes sensing ... [but] normal everyday perception and sensing are associated with a particular psychological set and content of thought ...in terms of evaluation of and action directed towards the external world. [58]

As, in this televisual age, he has fittingly said elsewhere:

> we can see how it would be possible to receive all one's visual information via a television set built around one's head from birth, and yet remain perfectly au fait with a [physical] world one had never seen 'directly'.

We should 'distinguish at all times

> between what is going on in everyday perception and what is going on when

philosophers and psychologists try to analyse and explain perception, their own and other people's. In the former case we do not consider ourselves to be using any hypothetico-deductive method or entertaining any 'theory of the world'. We simply get on with our seeing, thinking and doing. [59]

Removing the patina of theory that lies like a crust on what should be clear to view is a kind of 'scraping' of our own acquaintance: it is a way of becoming more intimate with what we are, as well as better equipped to test an intuitive self-image of a creatively active and single self-conscious subject, something we find no difficulty not just in *imagining* ourselves being but even feel that we are.

## WITH THE BEGINNING

There is no suggestion here that modern scientists are trying to chart the bed of a murky canal with a barge pole whose only empirical contact with reality is its measurable movements on an opaque surface. It is rather that they are ill-disposed professionally and theoretically to look into the wielding and its circumstances. For most purposes they needn't bother: what they measure in the light of day or on the laboratory's plasma screen is physical reality. A chunk of granite seen in that light can be investigated for what it is. Yet the light itself still waits to be examined, not in its abstract guise as pre-phenomenal waves, but as what envelops us in our conscious lives and puts on the display that is the world as we know it.

Acknowledging this fact, interest takes its evolutionary turn and looks 'back' at those small creatures in which the first glimmer of consciousness can be found in their ability to distinguish between light and darkness – and before acquiring that ability darkness would of course mean nothing to them.

It is fascinating to think that our present powers of discrimination can have this descent. However, not all neuroscientists have agreed that the descending (also in another sense an ascent) is straightforwardly continuous. As an early pioneer put it, 'I feel pain, I am delighted, I taste something sweet, smell the scent of roses, hear the sound of an organ, see red', but all this is a matter of 'perfect indifference' to the actual and possible positions of movements of a 'number of atoms of carbon, hydrogen, oxygen, etc.' It would indeed be a 'lofty triumph' were science able just to *correlate* mental with physical phenomena. We could then marvel at the way in which the 'play of carbon, hydrogen, nitrogen, oxygen, and phosphorus corresponds to the bliss of hearing music', and at how the 'whirl of such atoms answers to the climax of sensual enjoyment'. We could, at the other end of the hedonic scale, wonder at the 'molecular storm' that coincides with 'the raging pain of trigeminal neuralgia'. Yet none of this would help, since 'no imaginable movement of material particles could ever transport us into the realm of consciousness'. [60]

Following immediately the hearing of the sound of the organ and seeing red, comes a Cartesian addendum: the 'certainty' that lets us say: '*Therefore I am*'.

Advances in neuroscience since then have led correlators and 'connectionists' to discover ever more parallels between kinds of experience and states of the brain. Ideally, the full chart will display a total dependency of conscious life on the brain in every aspect. As noted, some brave souls (as with disarming humour they may still style themselves) claim that the brain can already in principle tell us all we need to know. Ever keen to cover the front line, journalists tend to feed a credulous public with unedited versions of current research's usually more reserved 'findings'. We are 'wired' for depression, for happiness, for unsocial behaviour, for religious feeling. Yes, the brain does this, the brain does that. As with DNA and the gene, a new folk psychology but with less secure backing is being born in which old popular notions are translated into neurobabble.

It will be a historical moment indeed for the connectionists, should they one day find a neural correlate of 'I am'. But until then, its absence may be left to the general mystery of how a physical universe actually puts on the phenomenal gloss that makes it our world. In this respect, connectionists seem less willing to jump the gun from the start than identity theorists; at least they seem happy to let the actual connection look after itself.

In this sensory version of Descartes's 'Therefore, I am', the 'I' looks like being an irreducible remainder as with Aristotle's *nous*. That same iconoclastic nineteenth-century pioneer pointed out that even if the 'atoms' of the brain knew *they* existed, the way in which their combined action resulted in consciousness would still exceed anything we can fathom. [61] He concluded that '[i]n a world made up of matter in motion the movements of the cerebral molecules are like a dumb show.' [62]

Equally dumb would be the show of other people's movements and sounds – what they say and do – without a shared repertoire of habits and a common language. But just as these are not enough to eclipse the need to refer to personal experience, so too our understanding of this experience requires something more than a parallelism in which every aspect of experience must have its corresponding physical cause.

In brief, instead of uncritically assuming that they are situated unproblematically *in medias res*, scientists might do us a favour and take a closer look at what questions being in the midst of things brings along. Begin *with* the beginning, not just in it. As for the philosophers, let them follow the example of their predecessors and consider how thinking can be more than a matter of bringing formal order to a 'world as we know it'. Better, let them open their minds again to the idea that when combined with perception, thought can draw out truths of universal interest from within and about experience.

# NOTES AND REFERENCES

1 David Hume, *Dialogues Concerning Natural Religion,* ed. and intro. Henry D. Aiken. New York: Hafner Publications, 1969, p. 7. The point is made officially not by Hume but by Cleanthes.

2 Francis Galton, 'Statistics of Mental Imagery', *Mind* 3 (1880), pp. 301-318 (see W. F. Brewer and M. Schommer-Atkins, *Review of General Psychology* 10 [2006], 2, pp. 130-146.

3 See Andy Clark, *Supersizing the Mind: Embodiment, Action, and Cognitive Extension*, Oxford: Oxford University Press, 2008.

4 W. V. O. Quine, 'Epistemology Naturalized', in E. Sosa and J. Kim (ed.), *Epistemology: An Anthology.* Malden, MA: Blackwell Publishing, 2004, pp. 292–300.

5 Ludwig Wittgenstein, *Tractatus Logico-Philosophicus* (1922), trans. C. K. Ogden, with intro. by Bertrand Russell, Mineola, NY: Dover Publications, 1999.

6 As in W. V. O. Quine, *Word and Object,* Boston, MA: M.I.T. Press 1960.

7 G. Frege, 'The Thought,' trans. A. M. and M. Quinton in P. F. Strawson (ed.), *Philosophical Logic,* Oxford: Oxford University Press, 1967, p. 35.

8 *Translations from the Philosophical Writings of Gottlob Frege,* by P. Geach and M. Black, Oxford:,Blackwell, 1952, pp. 79 and 60. Frege was reacting to the 'psychologism' of his day, in which philosophical problems traditionally conceived as an investigation of the a priori were tackled as if their solutions could be found by empirical (*a posteriori*) research.

9 For Kant, spying on 'the involuntary course of one's thoughts and feelings' was not only of no use in determining the necessary conditions of structured experience (or just 'experience'), it was also bad for one's mental health. See Immanuel Kant, *Anthropology from a Pragmatic Point of View* (1798), ed. Robert B. Louden, intro. Manfred Kuehn, Cambridge: Cambridge University Press, 2006, p. 22.

10  See V. C. Aldrich, 'Aesthetic Perception and Objectivity', *British Journal of Aesthetics*, 1978, No. 3, and 'Picture Space', *Philosophical Review*, 67, 1958, No. 3.

11  As in Gilbert Ryle's classic *The Concept of Mind*, London: Hutchinson's Universal Library, 1955 (1949).

12  The early Daniel C. Dennett, who in Rylean style referred to mental images as hitherto un-exorcised 'ghostly snapshots'. Dennett's, *Content and Consciousness*, London: Routledge & Kegan Paul, 1969, p. 132.

13  See John R. Smythies, 'The Experience and Description of the Human Body', *Brain*, 76, 1953, p. 134.

14 Charles Sherrington, *Man on His Nature*, Cambridge: Cambridge University Press, 1950, quoted in Smythies, ibid., p. 134.

15  Colin McGinn, 'Can We Solve the Mind-Body Problem?', *Mind* 98 (1989), p. 349.

16  By William Grey Walter, 'Features in the Electrophysiology of Mental Mechanisms', *Perspectives in Neuropsychology*, ed. D. Richter, London: Lewis, 1950, pp. 67-94. Also supported by John Smythies in correspondence with Francis Crick (23 Sept. 1994) who denies its credibility.

17  M. Charlesworth, 'Sense-impressions: a New Model', *Mind*, 88 (1979), pp. 22-44.

18 John Smythies, 'The Impact of Contemporary Neuroscience and Introspection Psychology on the Philosophy of Perception', in E. Wright (ed.), *The New Representationalisms*, Aldershot: Avebury, 1997, pp. 208-209.

19  Smythies, *The Impact*, ibid., p. 210.

20 Epigraph to Thomas Duddy's *Mind, Self and Interiority,* Aldershot: Avebury 1995.

21 H. H. Price, *Perception*, London: Methuen, 1950, quoted in John Smythies, 'Wittgenstein's Theory of Private Objects in the Light of Recent Developments in Neuroscience: with a Note on Asperger's Syndrome', unpubl. paper, Center for Brain and Cognition, University of California, San Diego and Institute of Neurology, University College, London; see also John Smythies, 'Brain and Consciousness: The Ghost in the Machines',*Journal of Scientific Exploration*, vol. 23, No. 1, 2000, pp. 37-50; 'Consciousness and its Brain: A New Paradigm', *The Psychological Channel* [thepsychologicalchannel.com – posted 7 August, 2008), and John R. Smythies, 'The Impact of Contemporary Neuroscience and Introspection Psychology on the Philosophy of Perception,' op. cit., p 222.

22 In correspondence to John Smythies from Francis Crick.

23 Larry Bird, legendary basketball player and coach.

24 Hubert L. Dreyfus and Stuart E. Dreyfus, 'Towards a Phenomenology of Ethical Expertise', *Human Studies*, Springer Verlag, vol. 14, No. 4, 1991, pp. 229-250.

25 Ludwig Wittgenstein, *Philosophical Investigations*, trans. G. E. M. Anscombe, Oxford: Blackwell, 2nd ed. 1958, §§179 and 180, pp. 72-73e.

26 William James, *The Principles of Psychology*, London: Constable, 1950, I, p. 631, emphasis removed.

27 Cf. Alastair Hannay, *Human Consciousness*, London/New York, 1990, pp. 75-76.

28 See David Woodruff Smith, 'The Structure of (Self-) Consciousness', *Topoi* 5 (1986), pp. 149-156; see p. 151: 'In this experience I see this [green] frog.'

29 Hubert L. Dreyfus and Stuart E. Dreyfus, 'Making a Mind vs. Moulding the Brain: AI Back at a Branch Point', *Daedalus* 117, 1988, p. 32.

30 Patricia Smith Churchland and Terrence J. Sejnowski, 'Neural Representation and Neural Computation', in William G. Lycan (ed.), *Mind and Cognition: A Reader*, Oxford: Blackwell, 1990, p. 230.

31 William James, 'The Experience of Activity', *Essays in Radical Empiricism*, London: Longmans, Green & Co, 1912, pp. 183f., cf. p. 158.

32 Ludwig Wittgenstein, *Zettel* [Note], trans. G. E. M. Anscombe, Oxford: Blackwell, 1967, §§ 610 and 611.

33 Henri Ey, *Consciousness. A Phenomenological Study of Being Conscious and Becoming Conscious*, trans. John H. Flodstrom, Bloomington, IN: Indiana University Press, 1978, p. 135.

34 From a draft transcript of the Jacobsen lecture, 'The Evolution of Consciousness', given by Daniel Dennett at the University of London, 13 May 1988.

35 ibid.

36 ibid.

37 Douglas R. Hofstadter and Daniel C. Dennett (eds.), *The Mind's I: Fantasies and Reflections on Self and Soul*, Brighton: Harvester Press,1981, p. 191.

38 Hofstadter, from a transcript of a talk given at the Christian Michaelsen Institute, Bergen, Norway, in October 1990, cited in Hannay, 'Control from the Top', *Nordisk AI Magasin*, vol. 7, 1992, no. 1, p. 38.

39 T. Hobbes, *Leviathan*, ed. and abridged with introduction by John Plamenatz, London: Collins, 1962, p. 64.

40 See Raymond B. Cattell, 'Theory of Fluid and Crystallized Intelligence: A Critical Experiment', *Journal of Educational Psychology* 54 (1963), pp. 1-22; *Abilities: Their Structure, Growth, and Action*, New York: Houghton Mifflin, 1971.

41 Marcel Proust, *Á la recherche du temps perdu*, Paris: Gallimard (Quarto), 1999, 'Le temps retrouvé', pp. 2272. See *In Search of Lost Time*, vol. 7, 'Time Regained', trans. (rev. D. J. Enright) Andreas Mayor and Terrence Kilmartin, London: Chatto & Windus, Modern Library Paperback ed., 2003, p. 276.

42 Immanuel Kant, *The Critique of Pure Reason*, trans. Norman Kemp Smith, London: Palgrave Macmillan, 2007, p. 29 (original emphasis removed, emphasis added).

43 J. P. Sartre, *L'Etre et le Néant*, Paris: Gallimard, 1943, pp 30-34 (*Being and Nothingness*, tr. Hazel Barnes, New York: Philosophical Library, 1956; London: Methuen, 1957, p. lxii-lxvii)

44 Werner Heisenberg, 'Goethe's and Newton's Doctrine of Colours in the Light of Modern Physics', *Scientiae Studia* 13 (2015) 1, pp. 207-221. Charles Sherrington wrote that, having appeared in 1810, Newton's *Opticks* had made *Zur Farbenlehre* already a century out of date (*Goethe on Nature and Science*, Cambridge: Cambridge University Press, 1949, p. 28).

45 J. W. Goethe, *Italian Journey*, trans. W. H. Auden and Elizabeth Mayer, London: Collins, 1962, p. 251.

46 Erwin Straus, 'Psychiatry and Philosophy', Erwin W. Straus, Maurice Natanson, and Henri Ey, *Psychiatry Universally and Philosophy*, ed. Maurice Natanson, Berlin/Heidelberg/New York: Springer, 1969, p. 73.

47 P. Basile and L. B. McHenry (eds.), *Consciousness, Reality and Value: Essays in Honour of T. L. S. Sprigge*, Frankfurt/Paris/Lancaster/New Brunswick: Ontos Verlag, 2007, p. 299.

48 Ibid., p. 311.

49 Ibid., p. 310. Sprigge adds that he is out to 'scotch the quite common notion that metaphysical attempts to prove the existence of God or of the Absolute ... are unfitted for promoting a religious orientation towards things.' (pp. 310-311) If such proofs imply knowledge, both Kant and Kierkegaard would demur. In Kant's case one must leave room for faith and in Kierkegaard's pseudonymous (and polemical) works, to argue for God's existence wastes time that should be used in following Christ's example. Sprigge may have seen his arguments, however, as providing support to an intellectual like himself for whom faith is already a *desideratum*.

50 Among these in this case the materialism 'for which human and animal welfare and suffering are mere physical buzzings in the brain much like the workings of a computer' (p. 311).

51 Martin Heidegger, *Sein und Zeit*, Tübingen: Max Niemeyer, 1957 (*Being and Time*, trans. John Macquarrie and Edward Robinson, New York: Harper & Row, 1962).

52 Rudolf Steiner, *The Gospel of St. John*, trans. Maud B. Monges, New York City: Anthroposophic Press, 3rd. ed. 1962, p. 33.

53 Op. cit., p. 27.

54 Carl Unger, *Principles of Spiritual Science upon an Epistemological Basis. Three Essays*, London: H. Collison, 1930, p. 135

55 See Rudolf Steiner, *The Riddles of Philosophy*, Spring Valley, NY: The Anthroposophic Press, 1973, pp. 31-32 and 39-42.

56 Ludwig Wittgenstein, *Tractatus Logico-Philosophicus*, p. 108.

57 John R. Smythies, 'The Impact', op. cit., p. 209.

58 J. R. Smythies, 'The Problems of Perception', review, *British Journal for the Philosophy of Science*, vol, 11, no. 43, 1960, p. 229.

59 John R. Smythies, *The Walls of Plato's Cave: The science and philosophy of (brain, consciousness and perception)*, Aldershot: Avebury, 1994, p. 111.

60 Emil du Bois-Reymond, *Über die Grenzen des Naturerkennens* [On the Limits of Science], In der zweiten allgemeinen Sitzung der 45. Versammlung Deutscher Naturforscher und Ärzte zu Leipzig am 14. August 1872 gehaltener Vortrag. In: *Reden*, vol 1. Verlag von Veit, Leipzig, pp. 441–473. Here p. 457. See Gabriel Finkelstein, *Emil du Bois-Reymond, Neuroscience, Self and Society in Nineteenth Century Germany*, Boston, MA: MIT Press, 2013, p. 165.

61 du-Bois-Reymond, ibid., p. 458; cf. Finkelstein, p. 165.

62 Ibid., p. 460; cf. Finkelstein, p. 165.

www.ingramcontent.com/pod-product-compliance
Lightning Source LLC
Chambersburg PA
CBHW070149310326
41914CB00089B/649